Rocket Surgery Made Easy

THE DO-IT-YOURSELF GUIDE TO FINDING AND FIXING USABILITY PROBLEMS

STEVE KRUG

VOICES THAT MATTER™

Rocket Surgery Made Easy:
The Do-It-Yourself Guide to Finding and Fixing Usability Problems

Steve Krug

New Riders
1249 Eighth Street
Berkeley, CA 94710
510/524-2178   510/524-2221 (fax)
Find us on the Web at: www.newriders.com
To report errors, please send a note to errata@peachpit.com

New Riders is an imprint of Peachpit, a division of Pearson Education
Copyright © 2010 by Steve Krug

Editor: Nancy Davis
Production Editor: Lisa Brazieal
Copyeditor: Barbara Flanagan
Design and production: Allison D. Cecil
Illustration: Mark Matcho

ISBN-13: 978-0-321-65729-9
ISBN-10:   0-321-65729-2

9 8 7 6 5 4 3 2

To my Aunt Isabel
(Sister Rose Immaculata, O.P.),
who has prayed for me
every day of my life,

My brother, Phil
who worked his whole adult life
as a Legal Services attorney, keeping
families from ending up out on the street,

And all the other people like them
who spend their lives
making sure that things work out
for the rest of us.

FIXING USABILITY PROBLEMS

THE ROAD AHEAD

Call me Ishmael

HOW THIS BOOK CAME TO BE, SOME DISCLAIMERS, AND A BIT OF HOUSEKEEPING

I knew I wanted to write this book nine years ago, right after I finished writing *Don't Make Me Think*.

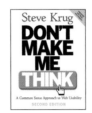

Without meaning to, in the process of writing it I had ended up convincing myself of three things:

- Usability testing is one of the best things people can do to improve Web sites (or almost anything they're creating that people have to interact with).

- Since most organizations can't afford to hire someone to do testing for them on a regular basis, everyone should learn to do it themselves. And...

- I could probably write a pretty good book explaining how to do it.

There was just one small problem, though:

       I hate writing.

Actually, I don't *hate* it so much as I find it, well, probably the most accurate word is *agonizing*.

And not "Should I buy the white iPhone or the black iPhone?" agonizing. More like red-hot-pokers-in-your-eyes agonizing. I've always said that writing is the hardest work I know of and that I can't understand why anyone would do it unless someone was holding a gun to their head (which, of course, is what deadlines are all about).

As it turns out, though, it was probably a good thing that I wasn't motivated to write this book right away, because one of the nicest side effects of the first book was that it gave me the opportunity to teach workshops, which suit my nature much better than writing or consulting.[1]

For the first five years, my workshop was a combination lecture-demo format, where I'd do brief expert reviews of attendees' sites to show them how I thought about usability problems. I wanted to teach people

how to do their own testing, but I couldn't figure out how to fit it into a one-day workshop.

Then three years ago, after a lot of pondering, I finally figured out how to do a workshop that would teach people to do their own testing—including some hands-on practice— in one day. I changed the format so the whole day

was about the topic of this book: doing your own usability tests.

After teaching this new format for a few years, I understood a lot more about what people needed to know. (It's true: if you really want to learn how to do something, try teaching other people how to do it.) And having watched a lot of people learn to do it, I was even more convinced of the value of do-it-yourself testing.

---

[1] *With workshops, you can't procrastinate: you either show up in the morning or you don't. And there's no homework. At the end of the day, you're finished. Period. The first time I taught a workshop, when everyone had gone home I remember having this very odd feeling that my work was actually done—something I hadn't felt in all my years of consulting. I highly recommend it.*

Finally, last year, in a moment of weakness, I gave in and signed a contract (and acquired the necessary deadline/gun) to write this book. After all, there are only so many people who can afford a day-long workshop. I like to think that reading this will be a pretty good substitute.

Does the world really need another book about usability testing?

I didn't invent any of this. Usability testing has been around for a long time, and a lot of people—Jakob Nielsen being the most vocal and influential—have been advocating "discount usability testing" for at least twenty years.

And there are several excellent books available that explain in detail how to do a usability test. I strongly suggest that you read at least one of them after you've had a chance to start doing some testing.[2]

But this book is a little different, in two important ways:

- **It's *not* comprehensive.** This book assumes that usability is not your life's work and probably not even part of your official job description. Since it's not, there's a limit to how much you really need to know and how much time you can afford to spend learning about it. As with *Don't Make Me Think*, I've tried to keep it short enough to read on a long plane ride.[3]

   The purpose of this book is not to make you a usability professional or a usability testing expert; it's just to get you to do *some* testing. Some of you will get really interested in it and go on to learn everything there is to know. Chapter 15, *Overachievers Only*, is meant for you. But you don't *need* to learn more than what's in this book to get enormous value out of testing.

---

[2] *You'll find a list of my favorites in Chapter 15.*

[3] *If you actually are going to read it on a plane, you should probably download the demo test video file to your laptop before you leave home, so you can watch it when you get to Chapter 2. You'll find it at www.rocketsurgerymadeeasy.com.*

- **It's not just about *finding* the usability problems.** Unlike the other books about testing, this one is about finding *and fixing* the problems. Chapters 10 through 13 explain how to decide which problems to fix and the best ways to fix them. This hasn't really been covered in much detail before, and it's kind of, well...important.

Call Me Irresponsible

Some people in the usability profession believe that it's irresponsible to tell "amateurs" that they should do their own testing. These are smart people, and I don't take their opinions lightly. Their two main arguments seem to be

- **Amateurs will do a bad job** and as a result, they'll (a) make the thing that they're testing worse instead of better, and (b) convince people that usability testing isn't valuable.

- **Amateurs will do a good job,** which will take work away from professionals.

Before I try to address these concerns, let me make one thing perfectly clear:

If you can afford to hire a usability professional to do your testing for you,[4] do it.

There's no question: a good usability professional will be able to do a better job of testing than you will. In addition to having experience designing and facilitating tests, a professional will have seen the same usability problems many times before and will know a lot about how to fix them.

Besides, it always helps to have a fresh pair of eyes looking at what you're building. And for the price of the testing, you tend to get an expert review thrown in for free, because the professional will have to use the thing to figure out how to test it.

---

[4] *...and it's not going to consume your entire usability budget doing only one round of testing...*

And then there's objectivity: being an outsider, a professional may be in a better position to point out unpleasant (and important) truths, like the fact that you've created a product that doesn't work or one that no one needs.

The problem is, though, that the vast majority of Web sites can't afford to hire a professional—at least not for more than one round of testing. And even if they could, there aren't enough professionals to go around.[5]

Even more important, *I don't think amateurs will do a bad job*. I haven't seen it happen personally. And for years now I've been asking for anecdotal evidence of cases where someone has made something *less* usable as a result of doing some usability testing, and I haven't gotten any to speak of.[6]

Not that I think it can't happen, just that I think it rarely does. And in most cases, I suspect it would be the result of someone pretending to do unbiased usability testing while actually manipulating the process to push a personal agenda.

And I also doubt that testing by amateurs will take work away from professionals. For one thing, it's not the kind of work professionals really should be doing.

Jakob Nielsen explained it perfectly in a speech about his vision for the future of usability at the UPA's annual conference in 2001.[7] He said that *everybody* should be doing what he called "simple user testing (debugging a design)," while professionals should be doing things that require more skill and experience, like quantitative tests, comparative tests, and tests of new technologies. Senior professionals, he said, should be doing really sophisticated things like international testing and developing new

---

[5] *Best estimates seem to be that there are roughly 10,000 people worldwide who would identify themselves as usability professionals, and only a fraction of them do testing for a living, while there are, at last count, umpteen billion Web sites. You do the math.*

[6] *In fact, I've been so impressed by the lack of response that I've thought about offering The Krug Prize: ten million Indonesian Rupiah (10,000,000 RIA, or roughly $1,090.16 US) split among the first ten people who submit reasonable proof of such cases.*

[7] *The UPA is the Usability Professionals Association (www.upassoc.org). If you end up deciding to really pursue usability, I highly recommend their annual conference. It's usually held in June, in someplace that's ungodly hot. But it's an excellent conference; the sessions are very practical (not academic), and the people are very friendly.*

methodologies (i.e., thinking deep thoughts and hobnobbing with their fellow wizards).

In my experience, people who have been exposed to testing almost always end up convinced that it's valuable. So I would argue that if more people are doing their own testing (and more people are observing those tests), there will end up being more work for professionals, not less.

Personally, if I had some money to spend on usability, I'd hire a professional to do an expert review and then do the testing myself. Or I'd hire a professional to do an initial round of testing who was willing to teach me how to do it myself.

Not present at time of photo

There are a number of things you won't find in this book:

- **Different testing methods.** There are many kinds of usability testing— qualitative, quantitative, summative, formative, formal, informal, large sample, small sample, comparative tests, benchmarking tests, and on and on—and they're all valuable for different purposes.

  I'll discuss some of these variations at the beginning of the next chapter, but you need to know that this book is only about one particular kind: simple, informal, small-sample, do-it-yourself usability testing (sometimes known as discount usability testing).

- **Ways to test instrument panels for nuclear reactors or air traffic control systems,** or any systems where people can be injured or lives lost if someone gets confused while using them. The kind of testing this book describes is not for making things *foolproof* to use; it's just for making them *easier* to use. For life-or-death situations, you want exhaustive, carefully designed, quantitative, large-sample, reproducible, scientific studies that produce statistically significant results. Or at least *I* do.

- **The one right way to do things.** There are many ways to do most of this. Where there are options, I've usually chosen the one I think works best for most people, or the one that's easiest for a beginner to do. But that doesn't mean I think it's the only way that works.

The obligatory companion Web site

Yes, there is a companion Web site (www.rocketsurgerymadeeasy.com), with files you can download, like the demo test video and all the scripts, forms, and handouts in the book.

These files are available to everyone, because I really do want as many people as possible to do their own testing. They may be updated at some point, although, knowing myself as well as I do, I have to admit that's pretty unlikely.

Maxims? Really? You're sure you want to call them "maxims"?

One thing you *will* find in this book is a series of what I'm calling—for lack of a better word—maxims. They're easy to spot, because they look like this:

 **Recruit loosely and grade on a curve.**

What are they? I suppose they're what some people would call critical success factors. In teaching people to do their own testing, I've found that there are really only a few things you need to keep in mind to succeed. But for some reason, people seem to have a hard time remembering all of them. So over time, I've reduced them to hopefully-more-memorable maxims.

If you forget everything else in this book, try to remember these; they're my most important pieces of advice. You'll find a list of all of them—suitable for framing and hanging on a cubicle wall—in Chapter 16.

A few words of encouragement

Four words, to be exact: *You can do this.*

For years, my corporate motto has been "It's not rocket surgery™" because I believe that at its heart most usability work is really not very hard to do. I have yet to come across someone who can't do a pretty good usability test—certainly good enough that doing it is much better than *not* doing it.

Since you're reading this, it's very likely that you're the *de facto* user advocate in your organization or department: the person most interested in making sure that your "product" (whether it's a Web site, a Web or desktop application, or whatever) is user-friendly.

You may not have much (or any) support for this interest. Or you may have moral support, but no resources. As a result, you're probably going to be pursuing it in what we laughingly refer to as your copious spare time.

But take heart, and be of good cheer: it's easy, pretty much foolproof, and you can start doing it next week. And one more thing people always forget to mention: it's fun. All the people I know who have been doing usability tests for years still get a kick out of it and find them fascinating.

So get started as soon as you can, keep it as simple as you can, and have fun with it.

FAQ

Isn't this just a rehash of your other book?

Who let *you* in?

No, it really isn't. The first book was about how to think about usability; this one is about how to *do* usability.

In some ways, this book *is* an expanded version of the chapter in *Don't Make Me Think* that explained how to do a usability test.[8]

It was very gratifying how many people wrote to tell me that they started doing their own testing based on the small amount of information that was there. This book, on the other hand, is intended to be a complete teach-yourself-how-to-do-it guide.

Chapter 9 from *Don't Make Me Think*

And besides, all of the headings in the first book were red.

---

[8] *At one point, I was a little concerned about the possibility of unwittingly quoting large passages of the first book without attribution and then facing the unpleasant prospect of having to sue myself for plagiarism. I think I've managed to avoid it. If not, I hope I can at least convince myself to settle out of court.*

What if I don't intend to do any testing? Should I still read this book?

Yes. Even if you're sure you're never going to do the kind of testing I'm recommending here, I think you'll find reading about the process—particularly the chapters about fixing problems—worthwhile.

I also highly recommend that even if you're not going to be doing full-scale testing, you force yourself to spend half an hour doing a very simple usability test of something that you're working on. If you give it a try, you may find that quick, informal usability testing is a great tool to have at your disposal.

Aren't you oversimplifying this?

Yes. That's the whole point. Doing this kind of testing is enormously valuable *if you do it,* and people don't do it because they have the impression that it's more complicated than it needs to be. So I'm trying very hard to keep it as simple as possible.

Does this work only for Web sites?

The focus in this book is on testing Web sites, because that's what most people are working on nowadays, and to keep the book short and uncomplicated. But the same method and principles can be used to test and improve almost anything that people use. Web applications and desktop software are obvious candidates, but I think it applies equally well to ballots, cell phones, PowerPoint presentations, instructions for digital cameras, and the forms you fill out in your doctor's office. I'd like to think that you could substitute "your product" wherever I refer to "your Web site."

How can you have "Frequently Asked Questions" in a brand new book?

Good question. They're the questions that always come up at my workshops. I figure it's safe to assume that readers will have the same questions.

1

You don't see any elephants around here, do you?

WHAT DO-IT-YOURSELF USABILITY TESTING IS, WHY IT ALWAYS WORKS, AND WHY SO LITTLE OF IT GETS DONE

Why are you waving that chicken around over your head?
To keep the elephants away.
Does it work?
You don't see any elephants around here, do you?

—VERY OLD JOKE

OK, before we get to "do-it-yourself usability testing," first, what is *"usability testing"*?

It's pretty simple:

> Watching people try to use what you're creating/designing/building (or something you've already created/designed/built), with the intention of (a) making it easier for people to use or (b) proving that it is easy to use.

There are a lot of different "flavors" of usability testing, but the one thing they all have in common is that they involve watching people actually *use* the thing.

This element of actual use is what makes usability testing very different from things like surveys, interviews, and focus groups, where you're asking people for their opinions about things, or their past experiences using things.

One useful way to categorize all the different flavors is by thinking of them as either quantitative or qualitative.

In a **quantitative** test, you're interested in *proving something* ("Is this latest version better than the previous one?" "Is our site as easy to use as our competitors' sites?") and you do this by *measuring things* like success rate (how many people finish the tasks you give them to do) and time-on-task (how long it takes them).

Since the purpose is to prove something, quantitative tests are like scientific experiments: They have to be rigorous, or the results won't be trustworthy. This means you have to define a test protocol and follow it consistently for all of the participants.[1] You have to collect data carefully. You have to have a

---

[1] *In usability testing, we call the people we're observing "test participants," not "test subjects," to remind ourselves that we really aren't testing them—we're testing the thing they're using.*

[13]

large enough sample of participants to make your conclusions statistically significant, and they need to be representative of your actual users so you can extrapolate the results to a larger population. All of this means you have to know what you're doing, and you have to be careful doing it.

In quantitative testing, you usually try to minimize the amount of interaction with the participant to avoid influencing the results. In an extreme form (sometimes called "Voice of God" testing), the participant sits in a room by himself with a facilitator giving him instructions over an intercom, while an observer watches through a one-way mirror and records the data.

So, what's *"Do-It-Yourself Usability Testing"*?

As you might have guessed by now, the kind of testing I'm recommending you do is at the opposite end of the qualitative–quantitative spectrum.

"Do-it-yourself" usability tests are definitely **qualitative.** The purpose isn't to *prove* anything; it's to get insights that enable you to *im*prove what you're building.

As a result, do-it-yourself tests can be much more informal and, well, unscientific. This means you can test fewer users (as long as you get the insights you need), and you can even change the protocol mid-test. For instance, if the first participant can't complete a particular task and the reason why is obvious, you can alter the task—or even skip it—for the remaining participants. You can't do that in a quantitative test because it would invalidate the results.

Basically, a facilitator sits in a room with the participant, gives him some tasks to do, and asks him to think out loud while he does them.

There's no data gathering involved. Instead, members of the development team, stakeholders, and any other interested parties observe the session from another room, using screen sharing software. After the tests are finished, the observers have a debriefing session where they compare notes and decide what problems should be fixed and how to fix them.

That's really about all there is to it.

The funny thing is, it just works

When I teach my usability testing workshops, I always begin by doing a live demo test—"live" in the sense that it's completely unrehearsed. The only preparation I do is to choose a site that belongs to one of the attendees and use it just long enough to come up with a task that I think people are likely to want to do on that site. (For example, if it's a health care site, I might make up a task about booking an appointment.)

Then I ask for a volunteer to be the test participant and spend 15 minutes doing an abbreviated version of a test. (Real tests typically last about an hour, although they can be as short as five minutes and as long as an entire day.)

The result is almost always exactly the same:

- The participant has a good time and gets a round of applause at the end for being brave enough to volunteer.

- The site's "owner" spends the entire 15 minutes furiously scribbling notes about things to fix and asks if she can have the recording to show to her team and her boss.[2]

- Everyone else ends up thinking, "Gee. Is that all there is to it? *I* could do that."

- When it's over, I ask, "Does that seem like a worthwhile way to spend 15 minutes?" and everyone nods their head in agreement.

The point of doing the live demo is to show people that (a) there's nothing to it, and (b) it always works. I can tell that some of them suspect that I'm able to make it look easy because I've done it a lot. But by the end of the day, after everyone has tried conducting a test themselves, they all seem to understand that there's no magic involved and that it really is as easy as it looks.

---

[2] *One "owner" wrote me a few months later to tell me that after viewing the demo test of his site, his team had immediately made one simple change that they calculated—based on the data from the first few months—was going to save their company $100,000 a year. (It had to do with getting customers to sign up for online billing.)*

I have to admit I was a little anxious the first few times I did live demo tests for an audience. But I've probably done fifty of them by now and it's worked every time, no matter what the site is and no matter who the participant is.

The fact is, it just works. Ask anyone who's done any amount of usability testing and they'll tell you that it pretty much always works. If you sit somebody—almost anybody—down and have them try to use what you're building, they'll inevitably encounter some of the problems that most people are going to encounter.

But *why* does it work?

It may not seem to make sense that something so simple (just giving people something to do and watching them do it) can consistently reveal serious usability problems. But if you think about it for a while (or for several years, in my case), there are reasons why it works:

- **It works because all sites have problems.** We all know this from our own experience. How often have you used a Web site and not run into a usability problem? And they're often significant problems that seriously frustrate you or even keep you from doing what you set out to do.

  Some mature sites may have fewer serious problems, especially if they've been through repeated rounds of usability testing, but don't kid yourself: Your site has usability problems. Heck, *my* site has usability problems, which as you can imagine is potentially quite embarrassing. Even Amazon has usability problems, and it's common knowledge how highly I think of Amazon.[3]

- **It works because most of the serious problems tend to be easy to find.** Again, think about the usability problems you've run into on other people's Web sites. Don't you usually find yourself thinking "How can they possibly *not* know about this problem?" Many of the most serious problems are lying around in plain sight, and almost everybody will run into them.

---

[3] *People love to email me about problems they find on Amazon.com, as though I could do something about them. I do have an Amazon Prime membership ($79 a year gives me "free" second-day shipping), but that's about the extent of my influence. And Amazon does so much usability testing that if there's a problem, I'm sure it's not because they're not aware of it; they probably just haven't decided what to do about it yet.*

And yet on our own sites, we somehow think of them as being hard to find. It always reminds me of the Vietnam-era Doonesbury cartoon where Phred asks the curator of a demolished Cambodian museum if it was destroyed during the secret bombings.

DOONESBURY © 1973 G. B. Trudeau. Reprinted with permission of UNIVERSAL PRESS SYNDICATE. All rights reserved.

The usability problems on your site may not be obvious to you, because you know how it works—or how it's supposed to work. Most of your users, on the other hand, don't, and that makes all the difference.

Of course, there are also serious usability problems that are more "hidden," the kind that not as many people will run into. But unless you have substantial resources to devote to usability (for instance, it's your full-time job), I strongly recommend focusing on getting rid of the obvious ones first. Most sites don't even manage to accomplish that.

And finally:

- **It works because watching users makes you a better designer.**
  Even though terms like "user-centered design" and "user experience" are now in the vocabulary of most people working on Web sites, relatively few designers, developers, stakeholders, managers, and check-signers—who all have a hand in the design process—have actually spent any time watching how people use Web sites. As a result, we end up designing for our abstract idea of users, based for the most part on ourselves.

Watching users makes you smarter about how people use things and how things can be designed for use. I like to say that it informs your design intelligence, sort of the way travel is a broadening experience.

Why so little of it gets done

So, if it's so easy and so valuable, why isn't frequent usability testing a standard part of every Web project? Even today, very few organizations do any usability testing, and if they do, they usually only do it once, near the end of the project.

I think it's largely because most people still haven't had any firsthand experience with usability testing, so they don't know how valuable it can be. But even if they have, there's no shortage of plausible reasons not to do it.

Lack of time, for instance. Testing seems like a lot of work, and most of us already have more on our plate than we can manage. Most Web development schedules are so tight that the prevailing attitude is "Let's get it out the door, and we can tweak it later."

And then there's the natural—and nearly universal—reluctance to show our work before it's finished. We always know that what we're working on has problems, so why bother showing it to people and wasting our time (and theirs) having them tell us what we already know? (And who likes having the flaws in their work exposed in public, anyway?)

These are all quite reasonable, but as you'll see, they're not necessarily true.

FAQ

You're talking about very small samples. Can't we get more reliable information from things that gather data about a lot of people, like Web analytics?

Yes, Web analytics can give you a very accurate picture of what people are doing on your site ("72% of all visitors left the Home page after less than 5 seconds"). The sample size is very large (all of your users, in fact), the data is based on actual use, and the query tools allow you to pose almost any statistical question and get an answer immediately. And with the advent of Google Analytics at such an attractive price point (free), this kind of data is available to everyone.

The problem, though, as any usability professional will be happy to tell you, is that while analytics can tell you in great detail what people are doing on your site, they can't tell you *why* they're doing those things. For instance, if people are spending a lot of time on a particular page, the statistics can't tell you whether it's because they found the content very useful and they're busy reading it or because it makes no sense and they're busy trying to figure it out.

Usability testing, on the other hand, excels at helping you understand why people are doing things.

When it comes to finding and fixing usability problems, if I had to choose between awesome analytics that could tell me exactly what my users are doing (but with no chance to know what they're thinking while they're doing it) or sitting with one user for an hour, with the ability to hear what he's thinking and ask probing questions, I'd take the one user every time.

2

I will now saw my [lovely] assistant in half

WHAT A DO-IT-YOURSELF TEST LOOKS LIKE

Is that all there is / my friend?

—REFRAIN OF THE ENNUI-DRENCHED
PEGGY LEE SONG "IS THAT ALL THERE IS?"

In the last chapter I described the demo tests I do in my workshops. Now you're going to watch one of them.

In most ways it's exactly like what you're going to do with your own site (or application or whatever). The main difference is that in an actual test you'd be doing more tasks—or longer tasks—so the session would typically last for about an hour.

Go to www.rocketsurgerymadeeasy.com and watch the "Demo Test" file.

1. (If you can't go online right now—for instance, if you're reading this on an old-fashioned airplane that doesn't have Wi-Fi access—don't worry; just go on ahead to the next chapter for now. But do make a point of watching the demo test as soon as you have a chance.)

2. While you're watching, keep in mind that at the end of the demo I'm going to ask you to make a list of the three usability problems you noticed that you think you would most want to fix if it was your site.

Is that all there is?

Yes, that's about it. No magic, no special skills. Some participants will run into more problems and spark more insights, some less, but on average you can expect to learn a lot from each one.

FAQ

So, if you don't mind my asking, why did you give this a whole chapter?

Because watching the demo test is important. I wanted to make sure you do it.

3

A morning a month, that's all we ask

A PLAN YOU CAN ACTUALLY FOLLOW

—HIGHLY SUCCESSFUL ADVERTISING SLOGAN
OF THE BLUE DIAMOND GROWERS
COOPERATIVE, CIRCA 1990

A s I mentioned in Chapter 1, people have a lot of plausible reasons for not doing usability testing. But the main reason most people don't do it is that they think it has to be a big production—what I refer to as the Big Honkin' Test.

While teaching my workshops, I've worked out what I think is a reasonable plan that anyone—whether in a large organization or a one-person operation—can afford to do and that will enable you to test what you're building several times during the course of a project.

It's doable, and it gets the job done. It uncovers as many problems as you can actually fix. And it keeps you focused on fixing the most important problems first.

I like to sum up my "master plan" this way:

A morning a month, that's all we ask.

Basically, it amounts to doing a round of testing once a month, with three users.

On testing day, you do three tests in the morning and then debrief over lunch. By the time lunch is over, you're done with usability testing for the month, and you know what you're going to fix before the next round.[1]

---

[1] *If you're in an Agile development environment, don't fret. See page 27.*

There are two important words to focus on here:

- **Morning.** Limiting the testing to half a day—which means testing with only three users—simplifies recruiting and means that more people can come and watch.

- **Month.** "Monthly" turns out to be a good interval. It's about as often as most teams can afford to do testing, and it identifies enough problems to keep you busy fixing things for the next month.

  If you announce that on the third Thursday of each month you're going to have people on-site for testing, you set up the expectation that people in your organization will show up to watch and that the development team will have something ready to test.

  Making it a routine eliminates having to decide *when* to test; you just test whatever you'll have ready on testing day. (If you have to think about when you're going to test, you're not going to end up testing as often.)

Do-it-yourself vs. the Big Honkin' Test

"A morning a month" isn't just about scheduling; it's also shorthand for keeping it as simple as possible so you do it often.

Do-it-yourself testing doesn't do everything the Big Honkin' Test does, but it produces the results you need at a price you can afford. Here's an overview of the differences (all of the moving parts will be described in detail in later chapters):

	THE BIG HONKIN' TEST	DO-IT-YOURSELF TESTING
TIME SPENT FOR EACH ROUND OF TESTING	1–2 days of tests, then a week to prepare a briefing, followed by some process to decide what to fix	One morning a month includes testing, debriefing, and deciding what to fix By early afternoon, you're done with usability testing for the month
WHEN DO YOU TEST?	When the site is nearly complete	Continually, throughout the development process
NUMBER OF ROUNDS OF TESTING	Typically only one or two per project, because of time and expense	One every month
NUMBER OF PARTICIPANTS IN EACH ROUND	5–8, sometimes ten to convince a skeptical manager	Three
WHO DO YOU TEST WITH?	Recruit carefully to find people who are like your target audience	Recruit loosely, if necessary Doing testing frequently is more important than testing "actual" users
WHERE DO YOU TEST?	Held off-site, in a rented facility with an observation room with a one-way mirror	Held on-site, with observers in any conference room using screen sharing software to watch
WHO WATCHES?	2–3 days of off-site testing means not many people will observe firsthand	Half day of on-site testing means more people can see the tests "live"
REPORTING	Someone takes at least a week to prepare a briefing	A 1–2 page email summarizes decisions made during the debriefing
WHO IDENTIFIES THE PROBLEMS?	The person running the tests usually analyzes the results and recommends changes	The entire development team and any interested stakeholders compare notes and decide what to fix over lunch the same day

	THE BIG HONKIN' TEST	DO-IT-YOURSELF TESTING
PRIMARY PURPOSE	A list of many problems (sometimes hundreds), categorized and prioritized by severity	A short list of the most serious problems and a commitment to fixing them before the next round of testing
RECORD VIDEO OF THE PARTICIPANT'S FACE?	Yes. Observers need to see the participants' reactions to things (especially frustration)	No. Seeing the participants' actions on the screen and hearing them clearly is all that's needed
OUT-OF-POCKET COSTS	$5,000 to $15,000 per round if you hire someone to do it	A few hundred dollars per round

FAQ

Can I really do this in a morning a month?

Well, no, not really; not *all* of it. What I'm saying is that the *testing* and the *debriefing* can all be done in a morning. And for most people on the team, that's all the time they'll have to spend each month.

But as the person running things, you'll have some prep work to do for each round of testing: deciding what to test, choosing the tasks, writing scenarios, recruiting participants, and getting all the stakeholders to attend.

The first time you do it, expect to spend at least two or three full days making all the preparations. For subsequent rounds, though, you should be able to whittle this down to two days, or even one.

Can I do it more often than once a month?

Definitely. A morning a month is just the minimum. Whatever you're building will benefit from as much testing as you can manage to do.

The important thing, though, is not to do it *less* than once a month. As soon as you stop doing it on the third Thursday of each month, you're back to making a *decision* about when to do it, which means that the odds of it happening drop dramatically.

We're Agile. A morning a month? Ha!

Ah, yes. Agile.[2] Given the short cycles in an Agile environment, if you wait a month the world will have passed you by. Perhaps it's more like "A morning a sprint, that's all we ask."

In many ways, do-it-yourself testing is an excellent fit with Agile, which is based on rapidly producing working portions of the product and getting them in front of users. The only problem is that in many cases these "users" are the team members who are doing the development. (You're going to fix that.)

Since you're going to be testing more than once a month, you may want to keep each round even leaner (two users instead of three, for instance) and do some of the rounds using remote testing (Chapter 14), which can save a lot of time. But other than that, the process is pretty much the same.

The biggest challenge with usability testing in an Agile environment seems to be that you need to be constantly laying out track ahead of the fast-moving programmers who don't have time for prototyping. (Everything they write is assumed to be working code.)

This probably means that you'll be spending part of your time creating prototypes of what they'll be building in the next sprint. So in a given round, you're likely to be testing what the team built in the previous sprint AND a paper prototype of what's going to be built in the next one.

Does it have to be a morning?

There's nothing magic about doing it in the morning. For instance, for some types of participants, it may be difficult for them to attend during work hours, so you might do tests at 6 pm, 7 pm, and 8 pm (providing dinner for the observers to encourage attendance) and then do the debriefing the next day over breakfast or lunch.

---

[2] *For convenience, I'll just keep saying "Agile," but you should imagine that I'm actually saying "any of the many popular software development methodologies characterized by frequent short development cycles and a higher priority on iteration and adaptability than on long-term pre-planning."*

The important point is to try to do all the tests in a single half-day, so as many people as possible can come and observe, and to debrief as soon as possible while the details are still fresh in everyone's mind.

What do I tell people who say, "But if you're only testing three people at a time, it can't be statistically valid. You can't prove anything that way"? Here's what you should say to them:

"You're absolutely right. Testing with so few people can't possibly produce statistically valid results. The samples are way too small to even bother with statistics. But the point of this kind of testing isn't to prove anything; the point is to identify major problems and make the thing better by fixing them. It just works, because most of the kinds of problems that need to be fixed are so obvious that there's no need for 'proof.'"

Try to say it with a lot of conviction and a friendly smile.

What's all this going to cost?

Here's an average budget for the out-of-pocket expenses (not including your time) for a year of do-it-yourself testing:

	Cost per item	Cost per year
Microphone	$25	$25
Speakers	$25	$25
Screen recording	Camtasia $300 PC, $150 Mac	$150-$300
Screen sharing	GoToMeeting $50/month	$600
Snacks/lunch for observers	$100/month	$1,200
Incentives	$50–$100 per person x 36 participants	$1,800–$3,600
	ANNUAL TOTAL (approx.)	$4,000–$6,000

And here's a "no frills" version in case you haven't got *any* budget:

	Cost per item	Cost per year
Microphone	$25	$25
Speakers	$25	$25
Screen recording	CamStudio (Open source)	$0
Screen sharing	NetMeeting (free)	$0
Snacks/lunch for observers	$100/month	$1,200
Incentives	Coffee mugs, t-shirts, or $25 gift certificates x 36 participants	$0–$900
	ANNUAL TOTAL (approx.)	$1,250–$2,150

4

What do you test, and when do you test it?

WHY THE HARDEST PART IS STARTING EARLY ENOUGH

I t's not hard to understand: If you're going to watch people try using what you're building, you have to have something for them to use. This means you have to decide what you're going to be testing each month.

People tend to think that you can't start testing until you have something that actually works—if not the finished product, then at least a functioning prototype.

But if there's one thing that usability professionals agree on, it's that you want to start testing as early as possible.

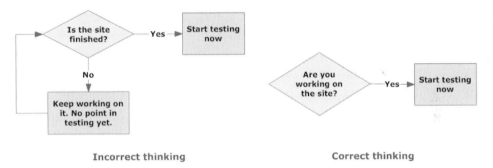

Incorrect thinking   Correct thinking

They know from experience that it's possible to detect serious usability problems very early in the development process, even if you have very little to show.

And they also know that it's usually far easier and less costly in the long run if you can fix usability problems early, before you've started building out the site with the problems embedded in it. Sometimes major problems that are detected too late can't be corrected at all. The worst practice is the most common one: waiting to test until the site is done and ready to launch.

Unfortunately, professionals also know that people resist the idea of testing early. Some common reasons:

- **"We don't have enough done yet."** After all, if it doesn't work, how can people try using it? In fact, it's never too early to start showing your design ideas to users, beginning with your first rough sketches.

- **"It's too rough."** Designers are often reluctant to show things that look unfinished. But users may actually feel freer to comment candidly on something that looks rough, since they know it's still subject to change.

- **"Why waste people's time looking at something we know we're going to change?"** During the design process, you always have a better version in your head than you've committed to code or paper. Yes, users will come across problems that you already know about, but there will also be surprises. In fact, you're mostly in it for the surprises: the things you didn't think of, because you're too close to it or because you don't understand your users as well as you think you do.

Here's the best advice I can give you about when to test:

 **Start earlier than you think makes sense.**

Your natural instinct will be to wait, which is the worst thing you can do. There's an inherent paradox: the worse shape it's in, the less you want to show it—and the more you can benefit if you do.

Throughout any project your team is going to be producing design artifacts: rough sketches, wireframes, page comps, working prototypes, and more. You can learn from testing all of these things, as well as testing your existing site and other people's sites.

In the rest of this chapter, I'm going to describe the different kinds of things you can test, how to test them, and what you get out of it.

Testing your existing site

If you already have a site and you're about to begin redesigning it, the obvious place to start is by testing your existing site.

HOW YOU TEST IT:
Follow the process spelled out in Chapters 5 through 9.

WHAT YOU GET OUT OF IT:
You'll learn a lot about what you're currently doing wrong so you'll know what to avoid as you redesign. You may even want to go ahead and fix some of the worst problems you discover. Your redesign is going to take time, so why make your users suffer until it's done?

You'll also learn things you didn't know about how people actually use your site.

Testing other people's sites

Before you've designed anything of your own, you can get a lot of value out of testing other people's sites. They may belong to your competitors or they may just be sites that have the same kind of content or the same kinds of users as you. Or they may just be sites that have features you're thinking of implementing.

Other people's sites are an underutilized resource. I always like to say that someone has gone to the trouble of building a full-scale working prototype of a design approach to the same problems you're trying to solve, and then they've left it lying around for you to use.

Most people overlook this opportunity, but it can save you an enormous amount of work. If you're building a travel site, for instance, think how much you could learn by watching people book trips on other travel sites.

HOW YOU TEST IT:
Follow the process spelled out in Chapters 5 through 9.

Give people the key tasks you test on your site. You may want to have each user do the same tasks on two or three competitors' sites.

But at the debriefing (Chapter 10), instead of determining the worst problems (since you're obviously not going to fix them), the team should have lunch and discuss what worked well and what didn't and what lessons can be applied to your own project.

WHAT YOU GET OUT OF IT:
The purpose is to learn from what others have done: what works and what doesn't.

As you might imagine, testing other people's sites has great appeal to marketing and management: they're always curious about what the competition is doing. It's a great way to get them to come and watch tests—and get hooked on the process.

Doing a round of testing on other people's sites can also be a good way to get your feet wet without any pressure. People aren't going to be defensive because it's not their stuff being tested.

Testing the sketch on the napkin

During the early planning stages of any project, you're likely to have some rough sketches or concept drawings, what I usually refer to as the "sketch on a napkin." (It may even literally be a sketch on a napkin or a placemat.) For a Web site, you might have a sketch of a new Home page or a product page, for instance.

It's always worth testing the sketch on the napkin.

HOW YOU TEST IT:
Napkin tests aren't full tests; they're like the Home page tour you saw me do in the demo test (see page 21). Each one takes less than five minutes. You can do napkin tests using friends, neighbors, or anyone you run into, or you can do them where your actual users gather, like a trade show or a user group meeting.

Here's how you do it:

1. Approach almost anyone.

2. Say, "Can you do me a favor? Take a look at this?"

3. Hand them the napkin. (It could be a nice neat drawing, or it could actually be a sketch on a napkin.)

4. Say, "Can you tell me what you make of this? What do you think this is supposed to be?"

Note that you're not asking for their opinion ("Do you like this?") or their feedback ("What do you think of this?"). You're asking them to look at the sketch and try to figure out what the thing *is*.

5. Listen carefully. They'll probably say something like "Well, it looks like a Home page for a site, and it looks like you're trying to sell __. And these things over here are your featured products. And it says 'Store' up here, so I guess I could order things online. I'm not sure what this category 'Incentives' means, though."

   If you want, you can ask a few probing questions, like "What do you think 'Incentives' might mean?"

If what they describe is what you were aiming for, get a bigger napkin and keep drawing. Usually, though, there will be something about the sketch that doesn't make sense to them, or something that they interpret very differently from what you expect, and you've learned something important without building anything—something you can now fix before you go any further.

WHAT YOU GET OUT OF IT:

You'll learn whether your concept is easy to understand—whether people "get it." They'll either confirm that you're on the right track or point out basic problems that you can then deal with early in the process.

I'll give you a personal example. For a long time (several years, actually) I wanted to call this book *Krug's Field Guide to Users*. The whole design of the book was going to be like a bird watching book: the same size and shape, and the same look and feel.

I thought it was a great idea. No, that's not quite right: I thought it was a *fabulous* idea. I loved it. Just thinking about it made me happy. I kept a rough version of the cover on the wall near my desk for inspiration.[1]

---

[1] *Actually, there was one title I would have liked even more:* The Junior Woodchucks Guidebook *(the pocket-size volume always carried by Donald Duck's nephews Huey, Dewey, and Louie that contained information and advice on every possible subject). But I knew that the intellectual property folks at the Disney Corporation wouldn't have been pleased.*

Then I did a foolish thing: I followed my own advice and tested it. The results were unanimous:

- Everybody I showed it to "got it" that it was supposed to be like a bird watching book. They all thought that it was a "neat" idea.

- They all thought that it would be a book about all the different kinds of Web users. When I told them that it would actually be about usability *testing*, they all went, "Oh...." They weren't upset that I was writing a book about testing. It just wasn't what the cover would have led to them to expect.

I couldn't see it because I was too close to it. I knew how it was supposed to work.

Testing wireframes

After sketches, the usual next step in Web design is creating wireframes.

A wireframe is essentially a schematic diagram of a page. Typically, it shows where different kinds of content will go, the relative prominence of things like headings, and the navigation devices like menus and search.

HOW YOU TEST IT:

You test a wireframe by making up tasks, usually all related to navigation: "How would you find ____?" "What would you expect to see when you click on this link?"

Wireframe tests won't take very long because there's not a lot people can do with them. You'll usually do them in a session which includes testing of other things, like your existing site or other people's sites.

WHAT YOU GET OUT OF IT:

The main thing you're testing is your categorization scheme and naming: Are things where people expect to find them? Do the category names you're using make sense? Is it clear how the navigation is supposed to work? You may find, for instance, that you've organized your site according to your org chart and users don't think that way.

Testing page designs

Typically, a Web site has a few unique pages (like the Home page) and a series of templates (like section front pages, article pages, and product pages) that are repeated throughout the site with different content. The next stage after wireframes is usually creating visual treatments (or "comps") of these different types of pages. Where wireframes focus on interaction, comps focus on the visual design.

HOW YOU TEST IT:

Starting with the Home pages, you lead them by the hand through comps and ask them to do a narrative (page 75) of each one.

WHAT YOU GET OUT OF IT:

The purpose is to try to see if the visual design has introduced any usability issues. Can people figure out how each page is supposed to "work"?

Testing working prototypes and beyond

For the rest of the project, you're going to have working pieces of the site available to test, ranging from prototypes to completed sections to the finished site.

HOW YOU TEST IT:

Follow the process spelled out in Chapters 5 through 9.

WHAT YOU GET OUT OF IT:

All the insights you need to improve your site.

5

Recruit loosely and grade on a curve

WHO TO TEST WITH AND HOW TO FIND THEM

Testing with one user is 100% better than testing with none.

—KRUG'S FIRST LAW OF USABILITY TESTING

And now, the boring part (for me, at least): *Rounding up test participants.*

Jakob Nielsen describes it as "unglamorous" and it really is: figuring out who to recruit, finding them, scheduling appointments, and getting them to show up.

I've never been fond of it myself. Maybe it's because it's the only part of the process that really doesn't have all that much to do with usability. Or maybe because I'm just not temperamentally suited to it. (It helps to be well organized and to enjoy talking to strangers.) Some people are very good at it, and some actually enjoy it.

But whether you enjoy it or not, if you want to observe people you've got to have people to observe. And like all the other parts of the process, you want to keep it as simple as possible.

It boils down to a few questions:

- What kind of people do you test with?
- How many do you need?
- How do you find them?
- How do you compensate them for their time?

Who do you test with?

When it comes time to figure out who to recruit, almost everyone instinctively has the same idea:

This seems eminently reasonable. After all...

- It's sort of obvious: you don't really care whether people who aren't going to use your site can use it. So why test with them?

- During the testing, representative users are more likely to experience the same problems as the people who actually use your site.

- People who aren't from your target audience will probably have problems that your actual users won't (false positives).

- People in your target audience may have domain knowledge[1] that other people won't.

It turns out, though, that testing with people who are representative of your target audience isn't quite as important—or as simple—as it may seem.

---

[1] *Domain knowledge is subject matter expertise about a particular field. For instance, real estate brokers know a lot about mortgages, property taxes, zoning, and so on. My favorite example is actually called "The Knowledge": to become a licensed London taxi driver, you need to pass an exam proving that you know 320 standard routes through London, including the names and order of the side streets you pass along the way, the traffic signals, and all nearby points of interest. People spend years acquiring "The Knowledge."*

Take domain knowledge, for instance.

Obviously, there are cases where domain knowledge and experience matter. For instance, if you're testing the form people use to order an industrial crane and they have to fill in fields like Span (feet), Height Under Boom (feet), and Capacity  (lbs), then you probably want people who know something about cranes.

But even where domain knowledge matters, it can be a tricky thing.

- Your audience is probably more diverse than you think. For instance, beginners often don't have domain knowledge, but they probably need to use your site anyway. If you're selling car insurance online, you probably want to focus on people who have cars and know something about the car insurance domain. But you also want first-time buyers to be able to use your site.

- People who presumably have domain knowledge don't always know what you think they know. For instance, years ago I was doing a usability review of a product designed for real estate agents. There was a term used prominently in the interface that I didn't recognize, so I asked the designers about it. They told me that every agent knew this term and used it often. Later in the project I paid the agent who had sold us our house to do a quick usability test for me. As soon as he started looking around the product, he pointed to the term and said, "What's this?"

And many of the most serious usability problems have nothing to do with domain knowledge anyway; they're related to things like navigation, page layout, visual hierarchy, and so on—problems that almost anybody will encounter.

I'm not saying that you shouldn't try to recruit people who are like your actual users. When you do need "actual users," by all means get them. I'm just saying don't obsess about it. For some sites you'll have no problem finding actual users, but for others it can make the process much more time-consuming and costly—and it's not always necessary.

Yes, there are things you can learn only by watching a target audience use the site. But there are many things you can learn by watching almost anyone use it. When you begin doing usability testing, your site will probably contain a lot of serious problems that "almost anybody" will encounter, so you can recruit much more loosely in the beginning. As time goes on, you'll want to lean more in the direction of actual users. But even then I would try to recruit one "ringer" in each round.

I also find that people who aren't from your target audience will sometimes reveal things about your site that you won't learn from watching "real" users, just because they have an outsider's perspective—the emperor's new clothes effect. And I'd rather have one articulate outsider with reasonable common sense who's comfortable talking than ten "real" users who are tense, quirky, etc.

I've had a motto about recruiting for years:

 **Recruit loosely and grade on a curve.**

What this means is try to find users who reflect your audience, but don't get hung up about it. Instead, try to make allowances for the differences between the people you test with and your real users.

When a participant has a problem, just ask yourself: Would our users have that problem? Or was it only a problem because the participant wasn't familiar with the jargon or didn't know the subject matter—a problem we're sure our actual users wouldn't have?

Three is enough

The debate over how many test participants you need has raged for a long time in the usability community, like one of those coal mine fires that burn underground for decades.

Almost everyone agrees that there are diminishing returns from having more users do the same tasks: the more users you watch, the fewer new problems you see. Most of the research that's been done—and the arguing—is about how many users will uncover most of the usability problems in what you're testing. For instance, "Testing with five users will find 85 percent of the problems."

But that's the wrong argument for you, the do-it-yourselfer. You're not interested in what it takes to uncover most of the problems; you only care about what it takes to uncover as many problems as you can fix.

After many years, I've settled on three users in each round of testing for a number of reasons:

- The first three users are very likely to encounter many of the most significant problems related to the tasks you're testing.

- Finding three participants is less work than finding more.

- It's much more important to do more rounds of testing than to wring everything you can out of each round. Testing with just a few users makes it easier to do more rounds.

- Testing with three users makes it possible to test and debrief in the same day.

- With only a few users, it's easier to encourage people to come and observe.

- In addition to diminishing returns, there's the tedium factor—for you as facilitator and for the observers. Starting with the fourth user of the day, there's usually a lot more snack eating, checking of voice mail, and side conversations.

- When you test with more than three at a time, you often end up with more notes than anyone has time to process—many of them about things that are really "nits." This can make it harder to see the most serious problems—the "can't see the forest for the trees" effect.

- Testing with a lot of users can uncover an overwhelming and dispiriting amount of problems. Prioritizing and triaging them becomes a problem in itself, another process to manage.

The easy way out:
Throw money at the problem

If you happen to have some money lying around and you don't have the time or inclination to do recruiting, you *can* make it somebody else's problem by hiring a recruiter.

These are the same people who recruit participants for focus groups, and the process is exactly the same. To find one, just search online for "focus group rental" or "market research" and your city. The people who rent focus group facilities will usually do recruiting for you even if you're not renting their space, or they can recommend someone who does.

The recruiter will work with you to define what kinds of people you're looking for. Then they'll locate possible candidates (either from their database or by some sort of advertising), screen them, schedule them, and even send them reminders to make sure they show up.

All of this is not as expensive as you might think— perhaps $100 or less per participant for the recruiter's time, more if the people you need are hard to find.

Recruiting is the only part of the testing process that I'd recommend outsourcing. But since this is a do-it-yourself book, let's assume that you're going to do the recruiting yourself. Here's how.

Where do you find them?

The first thing you need to do is think about where to look for the kind of participants you want. I think Willie Sutton's answer when asked why he robbed banks ("Because that's where the money is") says it all: look in the places where the kinds of people you're looking for tend to congregate.

For instance, if you want to test with senior citizens, consider senior centers, libraries, and church groups. If you want users of your product, try user groups, SIGs, and trade shows. (You may even want to do testing right at a show.)

If you want people who use your Web site, put a link on your Home page or create a pop-up invitation that appears when they enter or leave.

If you need "just anyone," consider friends, family, and neighbors. You don't have to feel like you're imposing on them, because most people enjoy the experience. It's fun to have someone take your opinion seriously and get paid for it, and participants often learn something useful that they didn't know about the Web or computers in general.

Testing with people who work for your own organization is tempting. They're right there, they're comparatively easy to find, and they're probably willing to help out. In a large enough organization, you may even be able to find people who more or less match the profile of your actual users.

But chances are they know too much. You certainly can't use people who work on what you're testing or people who support it, sell it, train it, or document it. But there may be people internally who know very little about it—people who work on completely different products or divisions, administrative staff, receptionists, people in finance or HR.

On the other hand, if you're testing your company's intranet, new employees are perfect. They're usually eager to create a good impression, they probably have domain knowledge, and not only are they *like* your target audience—they *are* your target audience.

There is one source of participants that I can almost guarantee won't work, although it may seem very promising: your marketing department's offer to get you a list of users. They mean well, but in my experience there always turns out to be some wrinkle: either someone in management decides they don't want anyone "contaminating" their customers, or there's a privacy issue, or something. All I know is I've never seen it work out.

If you're having a particularly hard time finding a certain type of user, consider doing some remote testing (Chapter 14). This usually makes recruiting much easier because it instantly broadens your potential pool from "people who live nearby" to "everyone who has broadband Internet access."

Put out an invitation

Once you've decided where they're lurking, you need to put out some kind of notice announcing that you need people. For example:

> We're going to be doing a usability test of a Web site on the morning of Thursday, June 25th and we need to find a few participants. It will take about an hour of your time at our offices in the Belmont area. We're specifically looking for people who have used online check paying to pay their bills.
>
> If you're interested and available on the 25th, send email to Larry Smith at lsmith@companyname.com. Include your name, phone number, and a good time to reach you.

Don't give your phone number or you'll be swamped. Scanning dozens of emails is much more efficient than listening to dozens of voicemail messages, and the people you want to recruit will all have email.

Where do you put it? Wherever you think people will see it.

- Tack it up on bulletin boards.

- Post it on message boards.

- Email it to your professional or personal network and ask them to pass it on to anyone they think might be interested.

- Put a link on your Home page or create a pop-up invitation that appears when they enter or leave.

In recent years, people seem to have had a great deal of luck using Craigslist to find participants.

Screen the most promising

Once you've got a bunch of people to choose from, you need to screen them. This means getting on the phone with them and having a brief conversation. In this call you're trying to accomplish several things:

- See if they're available on test day.

- See if they meet any qualifications you've decided they need. (Believe it or not, some people will stretch the truth to make a few dollars. You don't want to discover this on test day.)

- Tell them what to expect: the session will last for about an hour, they'll be using a Web site, you'll be recording the session (but not their face), etc.

- Explain how they'll be compensated for their time.

- Decide if they sound like a good participant. Do they seem like they'll be comfortable thinking aloud? Are they articulate?

- Make an appointment for one of your three test slots.

Follow up

As soon as you get off the phone, send your recruit email that confirms the appointment and gives the details: when, where, and what. Include things like:

- Directions (driving and mass transit) to your site

- Instructions about where to park

- The location of the room where you'll be testing

- A phone number where they can reach you (or someone else) on the day of the test or the night before in the event of an emergency

- Your nondisclosure agreement (if you use one) so they can read it before test day

Call them a few days before the test to confirm that you're expecting them and to answer any last-minute questions.

A hearty handclasp

Years ago I had a wonderful boss who gave me a bonus with a card that read, "Ever since the Phoenicians invented money, gratitude is no longer enough."

Sometimes it actually *is* enough. Some people, like government employees, aren't allowed to accept anything for being a test participant. And some people will be happy just to help you out, such as users of your product who are flattered that you've asked for their help or hope they can have some input into your future development plans. In cases like these, a gracious letter (not an email) of thanks will do.

Some people will be very happy with some kind of tangible memento—a mug or a T-shirt or one of your products.

But most of the time you need to offer people some reasonable compensation for their time, which includes the time it takes them to get there and home again.

Typical incentives for a one-hour test session range from $50 for "average" Web users to several hundred dollars for professionals from a specific domain, like cardiologists, for instance. It depends largely on what value the people you're recruiting place on their time. I like to offer people a little more than the going rate, since it makes it clear that I value their opinion, and people are more likely to show up on time, eager to participate.

Each method of payment has its own problems. If you give people cash, you have to get the cash, keep track of the cash, get receipts for the cash, and so on. Checks will usually require getting the participant's social security number and getting your accounting department to cut checks beforehand.

Probably the easiest solution all around is gift certificates. Amazon and AMEX seem to be the most trouble-free and popular.

Heir and a spare

If you've established a personal connection with your participants, most people will show up on test day. But at some point you're going to find yourself staring at your watch, wondering where the next participant is. Someone's car won't start, or they'll get lost en route, or...something.

And when someone doesn't show up, your observers will wander back to their offices and may not return for the remaining tests.

To avoid this, you should always have a substitute available. Depending on how loosely you're recruiting for this particular round, you have two options:

- **Just about anybody—someone who's going to be nearby anyway.** This might be someone you know who works for another company in the same building as yours or someone who works in another department.

- **An "actual user" who you can test with remotely.** If you need someone who fits a specific profile, it's usually unlikely that there's one sitting nearby and available. This is where remote testing (Chapter 14) can be a lifesaver, kind of like the "phone-a-friend" wildcard on *Who Wants to Be a Millionaire*.

In either case, the person needs to be "on call" for the entire morning: able to interrupt what they're doing on short notice and come to your office—or get on the phone—for an hour.

FAQ

With only three users, isn't there a possibility we'll miss some serious problems?

It's not just a possibility. It's pretty much a certainty that you won't uncover some of the serious problems *in a given round of testing*. That's why you'll be doing more than one round.

Can you use the same participants again in later rounds of testing?

For the most part, no. Once you've used them, they know too much, so you can't use them for later tests of the same site or application.

But you can use them on another site or another application. In fact, you probably want to, since you already know they're interested and are good participants. Pass them along to other teams in your organization.

I get the general idea, but I feel like I need more advice.

All of the general books on usability testing in my recommended reading list (page 141–142) have very good sections on recruiting. But if you really want to dig in on the topic, Jared Spool and Jakob Nielsen have both published excellent reports about how to do recruiting (page 143).

6

Find some things for them to do

PICKING TASKS TO TEST AND WRITING SCENARIOS FOR THEM

I f you're going to watch people try to use what you're building you've got to give them something (or some *things*) to do. It's a two-step process:

- First you choose the **tasks** to test— the things you want them to try to do.

> 1. Book an appointment online.
> 2. Find a gynecologist.
> 3. Cancel an appointment.

- Then you expand these tasks into **scenarios**—the little scripts that add any details of context they'll need to know to do the tasks.

> You need to book a physical therapy appointment for your 11-year-old son. It needs to be after school, and he gets out at 2 pm.
>
> Book the appointment online.

First, come up with a list of tasks

The first step is to jot down a list of the most important tasks that people need to be able to do on your site.

Try it right now.

1. Get a sheet of paper.

2. Make a list of five to ten of the most important things people need to be able to do when using your site.

For example, here's my list for my site:

> Get info about my workshops.
> Sign up for my workshops.
> Read a sample chapter of my book.
> Buy my book.
> Find out about my consulting services.

Go ahead, do it now. I'll wait.

Still waiting.

There. That wasn't very hard, was it? (You did actually do it, didn't you? You aren't just saying you did, right? Because if you are, you really should try it. It'll only take a minute or two. I'll wait.)

It's almost always easy for people to come up with a list of the key tasks for their site. In fact, when I ask an entire Web team to make this list, I'm always surprised at how much overlap there is across their lists. This is one thing they tend to agree on.

The trick is to make sure the tasks you test reflect your users' actual goals, not just your idea of what they want to do.

Decide which ones to test

Once you have your list, you need to decide which ones you want to do in this month's round of testing.

In a normal "50-minute hour" session, you have about 35 minutes for the participant to spend doing tasks. You might just have one long task or as many as ten.

People will work at different speeds, so you always need to have extra tasks for people who finish early. One good "filler" task is to have them do one of the tasks on a competitor's site.

Your choice of which tasks to test is based on a number of factors:

- **What are your most critical tasks?** These are the things that people *must* be able to do. If they can't do them, your site will be a failure. For instance, if you're selling books online, people need to be able to find books they're interested in and they have to be able to pay for them.

- **What's keeping you awake at night?** Things that you suspect people are going to have trouble with. That may confuse people. That aren't as clear as they need to be.

- **What does your other user research suggest may not be easy to use?** Have you asked customer support what kinds of problems they hear about frequently? What red flags do your Web analytics raise about possible problems people have using your site?

Make the tasks into scenarios

Once you've decided which tasks people are going to do, you have a writing job ahead of you: converting the simple description of the task into a script that the user can read, understand, and follow.

The scenario is like a card you might be handed for an improvisation exercise in an acting class: it gives you your character, your motivation, what you need to do, and a few details.

Task: "Apply for a doctoral program at Harvard Business School"

Scenario: "You've got an MBA, and after a lot of research you've decided to enter the doctoral program at Harvard Business School in Science, Technology & Management.

Apply for admission to the program."

A scenario provides some context ("You are...," "You need to...") and supplies information the user needs to know, but doesn't (e.g., username and password for a test account). Don't go overboard: trim any detail that doesn't contribute.

There's really only one thing that's hard about this: Not giving clues in the scenario.

You have to phrase it so that it's clear, unambiguous, and easy to understand, and you have to do it without using uncommon or unique words that appear on the screen. If you do, you turn the task into a simple game of word-finding. For instance:

> Bad: "Customize your LAUNCHcast station."

> Better: "Choose the kind of music you want to listen to."

Don't fence me in

There are two restrictions you may want to place on how people do the tasks:

- **Don't use search.** (Unless you're testing search, of course.) You will usually want to instruct the participant *not* to use the search feature when doing the tasks. If they use search, all you're really testing is whether the site's search is returning good results. If they forget and try to use search, you can remind them that you don't want them to use it.

- **Stay on this site.** In most cases, you'll want people to spend all of the limited test time on the site that you're testing. In most cases, they'll do this naturally, so I wouldn't bother stating it up front. Instead, I'd just mention it when they do stray, saying something like, "For the purposes of this test, I'd like you to stay on this site for now."

Pilot test the scenarios

Once you've got your scenarios written, you want to pre-test them in what's called a pilot test. The pilot test doesn't take as long as a full test: you can usually do it in about fifteen minutes. The purpose is to ensure that the scenarios are clear, complete, and unambiguous.

All you have to do is sit someone down in front of what you're testing, read them the scenarios and have them try to start doing each task. Anything that wasn't clear in the scenario will probably be obvious immediately. This is a case where you can definitely use almost anybody as a participant—in fact, this is a perfect time to use friends and family.

Usually you will do this a day or two before the testing. By that time, your scenarios are written and the developers and designers are [almost] finished producing what you're going to test.

Print them

Once you've made any final changes to your scenarios, you need to print them in two formats:

- **One per sheet, for participants.** At the start of each task, you're going to hand them the scenario so they can refer back to it while they do the task.

  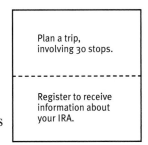

  Each one should be on a separate piece of paper, in fairly large type. I find that the easiest way to do this is to print two on a page, then cut the pages in half.

  Don't number the tasks, because you may want to change the sequence or skip a task.

- **All on one page, for you and the observers.**

7

Some boring checklists

AND WHY YOU SHOULD USE THEM EVEN IF, LIKE ME, YOU DON'T REALLY LIKE CHECKLISTS

I'm not really a fan of checklists. To me, checklists always imply a rigid process, and frankly, I'm much more of an improvisational kind of guy. But I am a fan of things that work, and in some contexts checklists work really well.

When you're running an event like a usability test, there are a lot of things that have to happen at specific times and a lot of small details to keep track of. Odds are you'll remember to do most of them, but checklists can keep things from falling through the cracks—particularly the one item everybody forgets: I can guarantee that at some point you'll forget to turn on the screen recorder, and you won't realize it until the session is halfway over. For some reason, this happens to everybody, so I've included reminders in the test script, too.

On the day of testing in particular, having a checklist gets these mundane details out of your head so you can be more relaxed and give your full attention to the participant.

You'll find downloadable versions of these checklists on the book Web site which you can edit to fit your own circumstances. (For instance, you may have to requisition the money for incentives a month in advance or order lunch for the debriefing from your in-house catering service several days ahead of time.)

---

[1] *Hence the old joke: Legendary director of biblical epics Cecil B. DeMille was filming a hugely expensive scene involving chariots, collapsing fiery towers, and thousands of extras, all shot in one take with a dozen cameras. When the action was over and DeMille had called "Cut!" he shouted through his megaphone to the camera supervisor on a nearby hill, "Did you get all that?" From the top of the hill, the supervisor waved back and shouted enthusiastically, "Ready when you are, C.B.!"*

Three weeks before

- ☐ Figure out what you're going to be testing (site, wireframes, prototype, etc.)

- ☐ Create your list of tasks to test

- ☐ Decide what kind(s) of users you want to test with

- ☐ "Advertise" for participants

- ☐ Book a test room for the entire morning with Internet access, table or desk and two chairs, and speakerphone

- ☐ Find a place near the test room for participants to sit and wait when they arrive

- ☐ Book an observation room for the entire morning with Internet access, table and enough chairs for observers, speakerphone, and projector and screen (or plan to bring a projector or large monitor)

- ☐ Book the observation room or a similar-size room for the debriefing lunch

Two weeks before

- ☐ Get feedback on your list of tasks from the project team and stakeholders

- ☐ Arrange incentives for participants (e.g., order gift certificates, requisition cash)

- ☐ Start screening participants and scheduling them into time slots

- ☐ Send "save the date" email inviting team members and stakeholders to attend

One week before

- ☐ Send email to the participants with directions, parking instructions, location of the test room, name and phone number of someone to call on the test day if they're late or lost, and the nondisclosure agreement if you're using one

☐ Line up a standby participant in case of a no-show

☐ If this is your first round of testing, install and test the screen recording and screen sharing software

One or two days before

☐ Call participants to reconfirm and ask if they have any questions

☐ Email reminder to observers

☐ Finish writing the scenarios

☐ Do a pilot test of the scenarios

☐ Get any user names/passwords and sample data needed for the test (e.g., account and network log-ins, dummy credit card numbers, or test accounts)

☐ Make copies of handouts for participants
- ☐ Recording consent form (page 153)
- ☐ Sets of the scenarios on individual pieces of paper
- ☐ Extra copies of the nondisclosure agreement (if using one)

☐ Make copies of handouts for observers
- ☐ *Instructions for Usability Test Observers* (page 94)
- ☐ List of scenarios
- ☐ Copy of the test script (pages 147–152)

☐ Recruit someone to greet participants as they arrive and make them comfortable

☐ Recruit someone to manage the observation room for you, and give him/her a copy of the *Hall Monitor's Guide* (page 99)

☐ Make sure incentives for participants are ready

☐ Make sure you have your USB microphone, external speakers, extension cords, and thumb drive or CDs for screen recording files

☐ Order snacks and beverages for the observation room

☐ Verify that no one has double-booked your test and observation rooms

☐ Find someone (your Designated Greeter) who can welcome the participants when they arrive, give them a comfortable place to sit while they're waiting, and then escort them to the test room when you're ready to start

Test day (before the first test)

☐ Order lunch for the debriefing

☐ Put observer handouts in the observation room

☐ Make sure whatever you're testing is installed on the test computer or accessible via the Internet and is working

☐ Test the screen recorder: Do a short recording (including audio) and play it back

☐ Test screen sharing (video and audio) with the observation room

☐ Turn off or disable anything on the test computer that might interrupt the test (e.g., email or instant messaging, calendar event reminders, scheduled virus scans)

☐ Create bookmarks for any pages you'll need to open during the test

☐ Make sure you have any phone numbers you might need:

Observation room: _____

Test room: _____

Greeter: _____

Developer: _____ (for problems with prototype)

IT contact: _____ (network or server problems)

☐ Make sure the speakerphones in the observation room and test room are working

Before each test

- ☐ Clear the browser history
- ☐ Open a "neutral" page (e.g., Google) in the Web browser

While the participant signs the consent form

- ☐ Start the screen recorder!

At the end of each test

- ☐ Stop the screen recorder!
- ☐ Save the recording!
- ☐ End the screen sharing session, if necessary
- ☐ Take time before the next session to jot down a few notes about things you observe
- ☐ If it's the last test of the day and you've been using a desktop computer, copy the screen recording file to a CD or thumb drive

8

Mind reading made easy

CONDUCTING THE TEST SESSION

Now for the main event: the test itself.

I'm assuming that you're going to be the facilitator: the person sitting in the room with the participants, giving them their instructions, and asking them questions. Eventually you may want to train someone else to do it too, but at least in the beginning you're probably going to be it.

In this chapter, I'm going to describe the facilitator's job, explain how to set up the test room, lay out the timeline for the test, and then discuss how you deal with participants.

What the facilitator does

As facilitator, you have two roles to play:

- As **tour guide** you're responsible for telling the participants what to do, keeping them moving, and keeping them happy.

    Unlike an actual tour guide, though, you're *not* going to be answering their questions about the sights (or in this case, the sites). The participants have to figure out how to use the thing on their own.

- As **therapist** your main job is to get the participants to verbalize their thoughts as they use what you're testing.

    This means that you're going to encourage the participants to think out loud as much as possible. You want them to do a running narration of what's going through their head as they use the site: what they're trying to do, what they're looking at, what they're reading or scanning, and what questions they have in mind. In other words, what they're thinking.

    This process, called the think aloud protocol, is the "secret sauce" that makes usability testing so effective.

I like to say that you and the observers want to be able to see the thought balloons forming over the participant's head. You're particularly interested in the moments when the balloons contain question marks or exclamation points, indicating that the user is confused, puzzled, or frustrated.

Whenever the participant's thought balloon isn't visible, it's your job as facilitator to ask, "What are you thinking?"

The combination of watching them use the thing and hearing what they're thinking while they do it allows you to see your site through someone else's eyes (and mind)—someone who *doesn't* know as much about it as you do. This is what produces design insights you can't get any other way.

The test room

For the test, you need a quiet space with a table or desk and two chairs—usually either an office or a conference room.

a Computer   b External monitor and keyboard   c Mouse   d Microphone   e Speakerphone

Here's what you need to have in the room:

a) **A computer with Internet access, screen recording software, and screen sharing software.**

The **computer** can be almost any laptop or desktop PC or Mac. If possible, I recommend using your own laptop instead of a desktop computer that happens to be in the room where you'll be testing. That way you can have the screen sharing and recording software fully installed, configured, and tested and know that no one is going to uninstall it or change your settings.

You'll need **Internet access** for screen sharing and to get to whatever you're testing if it's online.

The **screen recording software** is used to capture a record of what happens on the screen and what you and the participant say. The best part of having a recording is that you don't have to feel pressured to take detailed notes. By dragging the "thumb" on the scroll bar in the video player, you can usually find any point in the recording within seconds.[1] The recordings can also come in very handy at the debriefing session in case there's a disagreement about what the participant actually said or did.

In theory, people who can't come to the sessions can watch the recordings later, but in the universe I live in, it almost never happens.[2] I consider this fortunate since I'd much rather have people come to the tests.

I use Camtasia ($300 for the PC, $150 for the Mac). Even though there are less expensive screen recorders available (including one—CamStudio—that's open source), I don't know of another one that has as many useful features as Camtasia, including a built-in video editor that makes it easy to extract clips, add titles, and much more. I've relied on it for years, and it has never let me down. (Looking around for some wood to knock on.)

The **screen sharing software** allows the people in the observation room to see and hear the test. There are many options to choose from; some require a paid subscription and some are free, and almost all of them have free trials. If you work for a large company, they may already have a license for one of them. (WebEx seems to be a corporate favorite.)

Personally, I use GoToMeeting. It's extremely user-friendly and reliable, it works on Macs and PCs, and it has a lot of very useful features. It costs $49 a month for unlimited use, with up to 15 computers connected at a time. And it has VOIP capability built in.

It's also particularly good for doing remote testing (Chapter 14), which you'll probably want to do eventually.

b) **A monitor and a keyboard.** If you're using a laptop, you should arrange to have a monitor and an external keyboard. A 17" monitor will make it easy for you to see the screen without having to sit too close to the participant.

---

[1] *Believe it or not, this action actually has a name: "scrubbing" the video.*

[2] *To quote Yogi Berra again, "In theory, there is no difference between theory and practice. But, in practice, there is."*

The screen resolution should probably be 1024 x 768, unless you know that a large majority of your users will have it set higher or lower. (If the participant says something like "I have a lot more showing on my screen," you can increase it to a higher resolution, like 1280 x 1024.)

c) **A "plain vanilla" mouse.** Don't make the participant use an exotic trackball, a laptop touchpad, or one of those eraser-things that stick out from the middle of the keyboard that don't seem to have a name. Some people will find anything other than a mouse difficult to use.

d) **A USB microphone.** Getting good-quality audio into the observation room is crucial. Straining to hear what the user is saying can be very tiring, and eventually people will take out their BlackBerrys or just leave. Good audio also allows you to hear the "body language" of the user's voice so you can easily sense whether they're feeling comfortable or frustrated, for instance.

I recommend using VOIP (voice over IP) instead of a speakerphone if possible, because the audio quality tends to be much better. GoToMeeting includes VOIP service, or you can use a service like Skype.

You'll need a microphone to use VOIP. My favorite is the inexpensive (about $25) Logitech USB Desktop Microphone. Even if the microphone built into your laptop is good, having an external mike allows you to position it so the observers can hear both the participant and the facilitator clearly.

e) **A speakerphone.** Even if you use VOIP, you should have speakerphones available in both rooms as backup. (Make sure that you have the phone number for the observation room.)

Pre-Test Prep
Allow 60 Minutes

At the beginning of the day, you need to make sure that everything in the test room is ready. Try to start doing this an hour before the first participant arrives so you'll have enough time to fix anything that's not working, plus a few minutes to catch your breath when you're done.

☐ **Test the screen recorder.** Make a short recording and play it back.

The microphone volume setting should be turned all the way up since you and the participant are going to be relatively far away from the mike. In my experience, turning the recording volume all the way up won't distort the audio.

If you're using a laptop that has a built-in microphone, make sure that you're recording from the right source by tapping the external microphone during your test recording. (It should sound like you hit it with a hammer when you play it back.)

☐ **Test the screen sharing.** Ask someone to step into the observation room for a minute and then start a screen sharing session and make sure that they can hear you clearly and see the screen.

☐ **Make the cursor larger than normal.** This will make it easier for you and the observers to follow what the participant is doing.[3]

☐ **Turn off any software that might interrupt the test.** Email, instant messaging, calendar event reminders, and scheduled virus scans are the most likely culprits.

☐ **Make sure you have bookmarks for any pages you'll need to open during the test.** You don't want to spend valuable test time typing URLs.

---

[3] *I'll give details about how to do this—and the rest of my standard settings for Camtasia and GoToMeeting—at the book Web site.*

☐ **Try using what you're testing.** It never hurts to have one last look at your site or prototype to make sure that your Internet access is working, your server hasn't crashed, and some dedicated developer hasn't done some last-minute tweaking without telling you. It's much better to find out now than when the participant is in the room.

☐ **Reset everything.** If you're using sample data, make sure that you've reloaded a clean set. And clear the browsing history in your Web browser, so visited links don't give the user "clues."

☐ **Touch base with your Designated Greeter.** Make sure the person you've asked to welcome the participants when they arrive is ready for them.

Welcome
4 Minutes

You begin each session by reading the first part of the script,[4] which explains how the test is going to work.

Some people like to improvise these instructions from an outline so it will sound more natural, but I recommend using the script and reading it exactly as written. Even though I've been doing testing for twenty years, every time I give in to the temptation to depart from the script, odds are 50-50 I'll say something that gives the participant the wrong idea (using a word like "opinions" or "feedback," for instance). Don't improvise.

Hi, _____. My name is _____, and I'm going to be walking you through this session today.

Before we begin, I have some information for you, and I'm going to read it to make sure that I cover everything.

You probably already have a good idea of why we asked you here, but let me go over it again briefly. We're asking people to try using a Web site that we're working on so we can see whether it works as intended. The session should take about an hour.

The first thing I want to make clear right away is that we're testing the site, not you. You can't do anything wrong here. In fact, this is probably the one place today where you don't have to worry about making mistakes.

As you use the site, I'm going to ask you as much as possible to try to think out loud: to say what you're looking at, what you're trying to do, and what you're thinking. This will be a big help to us.

Also, please don't worry that you're going to hurt our feelings. We're doing this to improve the site, so we need to hear your honest reactions.

---

[4] You'll find the entire script—complete with "stage directions"—on pages 147–152, and you can also download it from the book Web site.

Read the script exactly as written.[5]

Reading it may feel a little uncomfortable because we don't often read things aloud—at least not to other adults. But no one will mind because the script explains why you're doing it, it's only about three minutes long, and they're probably curious about what's going to happen.

If you have any questions as we go along, just ask them. I may not be able to answer them right away, since we're interested in how people do when they don't have someone sitting next to them to help. But if you still have any questions when we're done I'll try to try to answer them then. And if you need to take a break at any point, just let me know.

You may have noticed the microphone. With your permission, we're going to record what happens on the screen and our conversation. The recording will only be used to help us figure out how to improve the site, and it won't be seen by anyone except the people working on this project. And it helps me, because I don't have to take as many notes.

Also, there are a few people from the Web design team observing this session in another room. (They can't see us, just the screen.)

If you would, I'm going to ask you to sign a simple permission form for us. It just says that we have your permission to record you, and that the recording will only be seen by the people working on the project.

Do you have any questions so far?

---

[5] *If you find that each time you read it you're stumbling over something that doesn't sound natural to you, you can make very minor changes that don't affect the meaning. For instance, if you think "If you have any questions during this session" sounds more natural to you than "If you have any questions as we go along," then edit your copy of the script so you say it the same way every time.*

Just try to relax while you read it and connect with the participant:

- Make eye contact. Print the script out in large type so you can read it without having to stare too intently at the page, and try to look at the participant after every few sentences.

- Don't mumble. The participant needs to hear what you're saying.

- Don't race through it, but don't drag it out.

- Don't read it in a monotone or a sing-song voice. Try to put a little life into it but don't make it into "The Midnight Ride of Paul Revere."

The Questions
2 Minutes

Usability test participants are often asked a series of pre-test questions at the beginning of the test and post-test questions at the end.

I only ask a few simple questions, and they serve three functions:

- **Get the participants comfortable talking.** Everyone can come up with answers to these questions, so it gets them started talking about themselves. This makes it easier when they have to start thinking aloud.

> OK. Before we look at the site, I'd like to ask you just a few quick questions.
>
> First, what's your occupation? What do you do all day?
>
> Now, roughly how many hours a week altogether—just a ballpark estimate—would you say you spend using the Internet, including Web browsing and email, at work and at home?
>
> And what's the split between email and browsing—a rough percentage?
>
> What kinds of sites are you looking at when you browse the Web?
>
> Do you have any favorite Web sites?

- **Show them that you're going to be listening to what they say.** Knowing that you're actually listening and not just getting what you need to fill in a form tends to make the participants more invested in the process and increase their comfort level. But to have this effect, you need to actually *listen*.

Feel free to ask them follow-up questions. I usually ask at least one question about their job, like what their title means or what their company does. And if you don't understand something they say ("We broker irreducible energy credits"), don't pretend that you do. Ask them to explain it.

- **Get the information you need to grade on a curve.** By the time the participant has answered these questions, you'll have a pretty clear idea of (a) what they do for a living and (b) how computer-savvy and Web-savvy they are. This—plus the sense of the extent of their domain knowledge that you get from their reaction to the Home page (coming up next)—is usually all you need to decide how this person compares to your target audience.

The Home Page Tour
3 Minutes

I always start a Web site test by having the participant look around the Home page and tell me briefly what they make of it.

The point is to see if the nature of the site is clear: Can users figure out what this thing *is*? As I'll explain later,[6] more often than you'd expect, the answer is a surprising—and revealing—"No."

> OK, great. We're done with the questions, and we can start looking at things.
>
> First, I'm going to ask you to look at this page and tell me what you make of it: what strikes you about it, whose site you think it is, what you can do here, and what it's for. Just look around and do a little narrative.
>
> You can scroll if you want to, but don't click on anything yet.

Having them do this "narrative" also gives you some idea of what they already know about the site, the organization behind it, and the subject matter—their domain knowledge.

Note that you're not asking them for their *opinion* of the Home page. The script doesn't say "Look around the Home page and tell me what you *think of it*." The instruction is carefully worded so they actually have a specific task to do: Figure out what this site *is*. This is a realistic (and important) task, one that people do on their own whenever they come to a new site. You're just asking them to verbalize it.

And it doesn't use much time, since most people will run out of things to say in two or three minutes. You don't want to let it go on longer than three minutes anyway.

The script tells them that they can scroll, but they shouldn't click on anything yet. If they click on a link anyway—and some people will—step in right away and ask them to go back to the Home page. Just say, "For right now, I just want you to stick to the Home page. Could you go back?"

---

[6] *The Big Bang Theory of Web Usability on page 122.*

The Tasks
35 Minutes

The tasks are the "meat" of the test.

At the beginning of each task, you'll hand the participant a copy of the scenario and then read it aloud, word-for-word, exactly the way you wrote it.

> Now I'm going to ask you to try doing some specific tasks. I'm going to read each one out loud and give you a printed copy.
>
> I'm also going to ask you to do these tasks without using Search. We'll learn a lot more about how well the site works that way.
>
> And again, as much as possible, it will help us if you can try to think out loud as you go along.

Why not just let the participant read it? If you do, some people won't read it carefully enough and they'll end up wasting time based on some misunderstanding of the task. If you read it to them, at least you'll know that they've heard every word of it.

Once they start a task, try not to interrupt any more than necessary. Basically, just keep them focused on the task and thinking aloud until it's time to move on to the next task.

How do you decide it's time to move on?

- **Have they completed the task?** If they have, hand them the next scenario and start the next task. (If they *think* they have, but haven't really, you can ask if they could try doing it again another way, which will usually lead them to realize their mistake.)

- **Is the participant miserable?** It's not unusual for the participant to experience a wide range of feelings while doing the tasks. With apologies to Elisabeth Kübler-Ross:

| Optimism | Thought | Puzzlement/ Confusion | Frustration/ Anger | Resignation/ Self-blame |

Making the user miserable is overrated. I actually think you learn less from a miserable user. (As someone[7] has pointed out, it's not a crash test; you don't have to actually destroy the car to see the problems.)

You don't need to stop at the first sign of a struggle, but if there *is* a struggle, you need to start thinking "Is this worth it? Is it causing the participant too much discomfort?" Always err on the side of the participant's feelings.

- **How much time do you have left, and is it important to get on to some other tasks?** Unless this is the last task in the session, you always want to be keeping an eye on the clock.

- **Are you still learning something?** My rule of thumb is this: when it starts to feel like you're not likely to learn anything more by continuing, let them continue a little bit longer and then move on. About half the time something useful will happen in this "overtime."

If the participant hasn't finished the task but you've decided to move on, just wait for a natural pause and then say something like "That's great. Very helpful. I want to move us along, since we've got more to do." (Note the use of "us" and "we" to avoid any suggestion that you're doing this because of some failure on the participant's part.)

---

[7] *...who I hope will identify himself, so I can give him credit...*

Probing
5 Minutes

While the participant is doing the tasks, you'll inevitably notice things that you'd like to know more about.

> Thanks, that was very helpful.
>
> If you'll excuse me for a minute, I'm just going to see if the people on the team have any follow-up questions they'd like me to ask you.

But stopping to ask questions tends to interrupt the user's flow and train of thought and introduces the risk of your inadvertently giving "clues."

That's why you always want to leave some time at the end to go back and probe. It's your chance to make sure you understand what happened and to try to figure out—with the participant's help—why it happened.

While the participant is doing the tasks, you can always ask for minor clarifications ("Do you mean the ___ over here?"). But for anything deeper—the "Why do you think you did that?" kind of questions—you need to jot down a note to yourself ("Didn't notice left nav" or "Chose second link. Why?" for example) and save it for the probing section.

Before you start asking your own questions, call the observation room and ask your Hall Monitor if there's anything the observers would like you to follow up on. (Feel free to use your own judgment about how to use the time available for probing, though. You don't have to do everything they ask you to.)

Typically, you'll want to ask the participants things like whether they noticed certain things and why they made particular choices. You can also ask them to try doing a task again another way, or from a different starting point.

If there are parts of the interface that you're interested in that they didn't get to in their travels, you can take them to specific pages ("I'd like you to go to the registration form") and ask them questions about them.

You may also want to follow up on any suggestions the participant made about features they think would be useful ("I wish there was a map to choose from instead of an alphabetical list of states"). Occasionally these can turn out to be great ideas, but for the most part they're not.[8] Users aren't designers, and they don't always know what they need, or even what they really want. Usually, if you let them talk their idea through, they'll end up saying, "But I guess I really wouldn't use it. I'd probably keep doing it the way I do it now."

Sometimes, though, users *will* make brilliant suggestions. How can you tell? Don't worry; you'll know. If it's really a bright idea, a light bulb will go off over your head and the heads of everyone in the observation room. People will say things like "Why on earth didn't we think of that? It's so obvious."

Wrapping Up
5 Minutes

Thank them, ask if they have any questions, pay them, and show them to the door. That's it.

> Do you have any questions for me, now that we're done?

At the end, I always like to say, "Thanks. That was exactly what we need. It's been very helpful."—even if things have gone badly. (Or especially when they've gone badly.)

---

[8] *Like the car designed by Homer Simpson with shag carpeting, two bubble domes, and three horns ("...because you can never find a horn when you're mad") that all play La Cucaracha, which ends up costing $82,000 to manufacture.*

Prepare For The Next Test
10 Minutes

Notice that I've suggested that each test session last only 50 minutes, not a full hour. This is like the therapist's 50-minute hour—appointments are scheduled on the hour, but they last for 50 minutes—and it's done for the same reason. To get

> Stop the screen recorder!
>
> Save the recording!
>
> Clear the browser cache, history, and visited links
>
> Open a "neutral" screen in the browser (e.g., Google)
>
> Take time before the next session to jot down a few notes about things you observed

the most out of each session, you need some time between tests to clear your head, gather your thoughts, and perhaps fit in a bio-break.

Obviously this means that you only have 50 minutes for testing. If you want to do longer sessions, you're going to have to get a little funky with your start times. But always try to leave at least 10–15 minutes of down time between sessions. Don't make the break too long, though, because observers will end up drifting away to take care of "just one thing" and not come back.

During the break, you should

- **Make a few notes.** It will all run together, even with three tests.

- **Reset the computer.** You want to restore everything to the state it was in before the test. Reload your sample data and clear your browsing history.

- **Consider making adjustments.** Based on what you've seen in the previous session, you may decide to make changes to the test on the fly. For instance, if the first participant can't complete a task and the reason is obvious, you can modify the task—or even skip it—for the remaining participants. You may even want to implement a quick fix to what you're testing if it's something you can do by making a simple change to a style sheet or rewording a heading.

Freud would be proud of you

Ever since I started doing usability testing twenty years ago, I've been struck by how many of the things a facilitator does with participants are just like the things a therapist does with clients. For instance:

- **You're trying to get them to externalize their thought process.** You want to hear what they're thinking so you can understand what's confusing and troubling them. Your primary job is to keep 'em talking.

- **You're trying not to influence them.** Like a therapist, you need to remain neutral. You can't tell them what to do; they need to figure it out for themselves.

- **You say the same few things over and over.** Many of the phrases you'll use are the same ones therapists use.

- **You have ethical responsibilities.**

Keep 'em talking

You'll find that some participants will think aloud with only an occasional reminder. For the people who tend to forget to verbalize their thoughts, though, you have to decide how often you should prompt them.

I used to think that it was a function of how long they'd been quiet: if they hadn't said anything for 20 seconds (or 30, or 40—I was never quite sure what the right number was), then you'd ask what they were thinking. But I finally realized that it's something else:

If you're not entirely sure you know what the user is thinking, ask.

Most of the time when the user is quiet, you'll still have a pretty good idea of what they're thinking. For instance if it's obvious that someone is reading something, you should just let them read. If they're making progress along a path that makes sense to you and they don't seem at all confused or hesitant, let them keep going. But as soon as you lose the feeling that you're certain you know what they're thinking, it's time to ask.

And you don't have to worry about it getting annoying. It turns out you can say "What are you thinking?" dozens of times in a test and participants won't even be aware of it. And if *you* get bored saying it, you can mix it up with "What are you looking at?" and "What are you doing?"—both of which have about the same effect.

Stay neutral

Like a therapist, one of the hardest parts of your job as facilitator is staying neutral: you don't want to influence the participants.

The worst case is when the facilitator is actively trying to advance a personal agenda, either consciously or unconsciously. For instance, you may want to see the thing you're testing succeed because you had a hand in designing it, or you may want to see it fail because you've thought all along it was a bad idea.

As facilitator, you have a responsibility to be aware of your biases and scrupulously steer clear of influencing what happens during the testing. If you don't, people will notice and your testing will lose its credibility.

But even if you don't have a personal agenda, you still have to do everything you can to avoid influencing the participant:

- You can't tell them what to do or give them clues—even subtle ones. When the participant is struggling, you'll want to help, but you need to resist the temptation.

- You can't answer their questions. You'll have to answer most questions with a question, like "What do *you* think?"

- You shouldn't express your own opinions ("That's a great feature"), or even agree with theirs ("Yeah, that *is* a great feature").

- You need to try to maintain a poker face, not giving any sign that you're particularly pleased or displeased with what's happening. (I think it's probably best to seem consistently *somewhat* pleased throughout—conveying the sense that the test is going well and you're getting what you need.)

"Things a therapist would say"

While the participant is doing the tasks, to maintain your neutrality you're going to be saying the same few things over and over. Here's a handy chart:

WHEN THIS HAPPENS:	SAY THIS:
You're not absolutely sure you know what the participant is thinking.	"What are you thinking?" "What are you looking at?" "What are you doing now?"
Something happens that seems to surprise them. For instance, they click on a link and say "Oh" or "Hmmm" when the new page appears.	"Is that what you expected to happen?"
The participant is trying to get you to give him a clue. ("Should I use the _____?")	"What would you do if you were at home?" (Wait for answer.) "Then why don't you go ahead and try that?" "What would you do if I wasn't here?" "I'd like you to do whatever you'd normally do."
The participant makes a comment, and you're not sure what triggered it.	"Was there something in particular that made you think that?"
The participant suggests concern that he's not giving you what you need.	"No, this is very helpful." "This is exactly what we need."

The participant asks you to explain how something works or is supposed to work (e.g., "Do these support requests get answered overnight?").	"What do you think?" "How do you think it would work?" "I can't answer that right now, because we need to know what you would do when you don't have somebody around to answer questions for you. But if you still want to know when we're done, I'll be glad to answer it then."
The participant seems to have wandered away from the task.	"What are you trying to do now?"

There are also three other kinds of things you can say:

- **Acknowledgment tokens.** You can say things like "uh huh," "OK," and "mm hmm" as often as you think necessary. These signal that you're taking in what the participant is saying and you'd like them to continue along the same lines. Note that they're meant to indicate that you understand what the participant is saying, not that you necessarily agree with it. It's "OK." Not "OK!!!"

- **Paraphrasing.** Sometimes it helps to give a little summary of what the participant just said ("So you're saying that the boxes on the bottom are hard to read?") to make sure that you've heard and understood correctly.

- **Clarifying for observers.** If the user makes a vague reference to something on the screen, you may want to do a little bit of narration to make it easier for the observers to follow the action. For instance, when the user says "I love this," you can say, "The list over here on the right?" (Since you're sitting next to the participant, you sometimes have a better sense of what they're looking at.)

Ethical considerations

There's one final thing you have in common with a therapist: you have an ethical responsibility to your participants. Like anything to do with ethics, this responsibility can be complicated, but I like to think it boils down to this:

Participants should leave the room in no worse shape than they entered.

For the most part usability testing tends to be very benign. You're not attaching electrodes to anyone, and unless you're a closet sociopath, I don't think you're likely to cause anyone serious emotional damage. I assume you're going to treat them with respect, empathy, and consideration of their feelings, even if they turn out to be a pain in the neck. (Perhaps *especially* if they turn out to be a pain in the neck.) In other words, you're going to behave like a decent human being.

The participant always has the right to stop the test and leave at any time without penalty. (You still pay them.) You should work to make the test as comfortable, unintimidating, and stress-free as possible, keep a close eye on the participant's comfort level, and be very gracious and agreeable if they *do* want to stop. In some rare cases, *you'll* ask *them* if they'd like to stop.

You also have a responsibility to protect the participants' privacy. One of the best ways to do this is to avoid using identifying information. There's no need to use their last names in the tests or recordings, and you're not going to record their faces.

You need to keep the recordings under your personal control and erase them as soon as they're no longer needed. If you're going to distribute clips within your organization, each one should begin with a scary-sounding FBI-style warning not to redistribute it, and you should redact any personal information like telephone or credit card numbers. (It's fairly easy to cover things up with the editing features of Camtasia.) And if someone makes a particularly indiscreet (or even incriminating) statement, you should delete that portion of the recording.[9] I would also never distribute clips of employees who were participants because it may put them in an awkward position.

If you're in an academic setting, you may be required to get approval of your entire test plan (including the script and an informed consent agreement) from your Institutional Review Board (IRB) to ensure that it meets your institution's ethical standards. But you can probably make a very good case that informal usability tests like this are not the kind of study that your IRB has to oversee. (People have managed to get this kind of exemption in the past.)

---

[9] *Carolyn Snyder has talked about doing this when a participant mentioned smoking pot, for instance. I was once testing a site with some college students (at a Catholic university, no less) and asked casually what kinds of sites a participant used. "Well, there's porn..." he began. I left this clip out of my presentation.*

Tough customers

Most participants turn out to be pleasant and productive. And then there are the less-than-perfect participants...

You may get a slow talker,[10] a no-talker, a low-talker, a fast talker, a nonstop talker, a know-it-all, or even (fortunately, very rarely) the occasional wacko.

Keeping some participants on task can feel like herding the proverbial kittens. Sometimes people will leave the site you're testing. Sometimes they'll get distracted by some bright, shiny object on a page or decide to tell you a story. Some people will want to talk about the economy.

As with kittens, you need to be polite but firm and keep them moving. For instance, "Good. *[creating a pause, and suggesting that things are actually going well]* OK. *[suggesting a transition is occurring]* We've got a lot to cover, so I'm going to ask you to...."

You have to be prepared to be persistent and a bit ruthless. It may feel like you're being rude, but remember that you're paying them for their time, and if you don't get what you need, you're wasting your time, their time, and your observers' time.

Even after you get them back on track, some will relapse. Bite your tongue but be patient. Someone who seems hopeless may come around and end up providing you with really valuable insights.

In extreme cases, if you're not getting any benefit from the participant, you may decide to end the session early. For instance, you may have someone who is clearly not qualified. Either your recruiting wasn't up to snuff, or they were deceptive when you spoke to them.

If you feel the need to end the session early, you can use any plausible (and hopefully convincing) excuse, thank them, pay them, and get ready for your next session.

---

[10] *Do yourself a favor and search the Web for an audio file of Bob and Ray's "Slow Talkers of America" sketch.*

Don't worry, be happy

Reading about all of this may make the facilitator's job sound like a lot to handle, but the truth is almost everyone who tries it finds it to be surprisingly easy. Most people get the hang of it very quickly, but it's only natural to be a little anxious (or for some people, very anxious) the first few times you run a test. Here are two things that can help minimize any stage fright:

- **Practice reading the script aloud.** First read it out loud with no one around four or five times, then read it to one or two people: a family member, for instance, or co-workers. By then you won't be self-conscious about it anymore.

- **Do a practice test with no pressure.** If you find you're really anxious about your first public test, try doing a "dry run." Get two friends to be the participant and an observer and do everything you would in a real test, including setting up screen sharing in another room.

FAQ

Who should be a facilitator?

Probably you. You've demonstrated interest by reading this book, and interest is the best qualifier. It certainly helps if you're a good listener and you're comfortable chatting with strangers. But as someone once pointed out to me, you don't have to actually be a "people person" to facilitate well, as long as you can *pretend* to like people.

As time goes on, you'll probably want to train someone else on your team to facilitate, too, so you can just observe and take notes. (As the person most interested in usability, your notes and observations are usually the most valuable.)

Who *shouldn't* be a facilitator?

Anyone who really doesn't like people—the office curmudgeon, for instance—is probably a poor choice. Also people who don't listen well, people who tend to be impatient, and people who like to force their ideas on others.

The worst choice would be someone who has a personal agenda about the right way to design things that they can't put aside.

Where should I sit? Next to the participant? Behind him?

The participant needs to sit directly in front of the monitor and keyboard, and you need to be positioned so you can see the screen clearly enough to follow what they're doing. I find that it works best if I'm sitting next to the participant and slightly behind, just far enough away so they won't feel like I'm hovering.

Should I take notes while I'm facilitating?

As you gain experience, you'll find that you can take some notes *and* pay full attention to the participant *and* keep the session moving, all at the same time. In the beginning, though, I recommend that most of the notes you take during the tests should just be reminders about things that you want to follow up on during the probing, like "Did he see download link?"

The observers will be taking plenty of notes, and if you need to you can always go back and look at the recording. But don't forget to make your Top Problems list after each session while it's still fresh in your mind.

Why don't you ask more entrance and exit questions?

Pre- and post-test questions are often used to try to assess things like whether people find the site usable and whether using the site improves their opinion of your organization or product. These can be very valuable and they certainly make marketing people happy, but I don't think they have a place in do-it-yourself testing.

For one thing, the samples are too small to have any meaning. And there's also the problem that people are notoriously bad at this kind of self-reporting. The biggest running joke among usability professionals is that we've all seen people who have struggled almost to the point of tears trying to use a system that just doesn't work the way it should. But when it comes time to rate it on a scale of 1 (user-hostile) to 7 (extraordinarily user-friendly), they'll give it a "6." We don't know why it happens, but it does. All the time.[11]

---

[11] *It may be because they think of you as their host—you've been nice to them and you're paying them for their time so they don't want to seem rude. Or it may just be that people*

You recommended Camtasia. What about Morae?

Some years ago, so many people were using Camtasia to record usability tests that the folks at TechSmith decided to build another product specifically designed for usability testing: Morae. I think of it as Camtasia on steroids. It has a ton of additional features, including a logging capability which makes it easy for an observer to take notes that are synched to the recording. And it has its own remote viewer which eliminates the need for a separate screen sharing solution.

It's a wonderful tool and a lot of people use it, but for the kind of testing I'm talking about, I think it's overkill for most people. I'd recommend starting out with the simpler tool and graduating to Morae when you have a need for it. In the meantime, you may want to download the 30-day free trial and learn what it can do.

What about recording the user's face?

I've never been a big fan of recording the user's face during testing.

The original purpose of this picture-in-picture feature (or perhaps more accurately, "pain-in-picture") was to capture the participant's frustration to use as proof that the product needed more usability work. But I think this "SquirmCam" can actually be an unnecessary distraction.

If you have good quality audio, observers can almost always tell what the user is feeling from their tone of voice.

---

have such low expectations that your site seems no worse than most. Personally, I think it's a variant of Stockholm syndrome, where hostages develop an emotional bond with their captors, sympathizing with them and even defending them after they're finally freed.

9

Make it a spectator sport

GETTING EVERYONE TO WATCH AND TELLING THEM
WHAT TO LOOK FOR

One of the most valuable pieces of advice I can give you about usability testing is to do everything you can to get as many people in your organization as possible (stakeholders, managers, developers, designers, editors, writers—even executives) to attend your test sessions in person. Or, in maxim-speak:

Make it a spectator sport.

Why do I think it's so important to get people there in person? Because, when it comes to usability testing...

Seeing is believing

It's another one of the things that everyone who's done a lot of testing knows: watching usability tests in person is a transformative experience. People often go into their first test with some skepticism, but they almost invariably come out...changed.

The most obvious change is that they're not skeptical about testing anymore; in fact, they're usually enthusiastic about it. It's hard to watch tests and not understand that what you're seeing is very valuable.

But there's a subtler and more significant change: watching usability testing makes you realize that your users aren't just like you. Most people think that all users are just like them when it comes to using the Web. Watching real users gives them that eureka moment: they're not all like me, and in fact they're not *all* like *anybody*. I like to say that watching usability tests is like travel: it's a broadening experience. You realize that the rest of the world doesn't live and think the same way you do. This profoundly and permanently changes your relationship to users, making you a better developer, designer, manager, or whatever you are.

For reasons that aren't entirely clear, this transformative effect is much more pronounced when you watch tests live and in person than when you watch clips or a recorded session. It's like the difference between watching a sporting event live on television and watching a replay later: "live" is just more compelling. And when you attend a session with others, you also benefit from the shared group experience and the opportunity to compare observations during and between test sessions.

Whatever the reason is, believe me: it pays to get people in the room.

The more, the merrier

When you start doing monthly testing, the people who are directly involved in the part of the site that's being tested will probably be eager to come and watch.

But you want to make a point of inviting and encouraging *everyone* to attend: designers, developers, product managers, bosses, marketing people, writers, editors, and all the various stakeholders who have interest or influence in the design and content.

Do everything you can to get people to come. A few things that tend to work:

- **Make it easy for people to attend.** It helps to schedule your monthly usability testing on a "slow" day of the week and at a slow time of the month.

- **Advertise.** Send out a "save the date" email two weeks before the test day that says what you'll be testing; then send out a tickler email a few days before the tests and a last-minute reminder the day before.

- **Make it clear what's in it for them.** Stakeholders are always interested in getting their "pet" problems fixed. Make sure they understand that attending tests gives them a voice in the debriefing where these things are decided.

- **Trick executives into coming.** I always tell people to do whatever it takes to get people from management to attend. Tell them that it will be good for morale if they could just drop by for a bit. I've seen VPs who "dropped by" cancel meetings so they can stay and keep watching. Dilbert notwithstanding, these are usually smart people who recognize the value of this kind of input once they see it firsthand.

- **Provide quality snacks.** Word will get around.

What do observers do?

The observers' job is very simple:

- Watch and learn, and take some notes.

- At the end of each session, write down the three most important usability problems they saw in that session.

- Suggest questions they'd like to have the facilitator ask the participant.

- Enjoy the snacks.

- Come to the lunchtime debriefing session.

That's it. Here's a set of instructions you should give them.[1]

---

[1] *You can download this handout from the book Web site and edit it (if you're doing longer or shorter sessions, for instance).*

Instructions for Usability Test Observers

Thanks for coming to today's tests. Each of the three sessions will last about 50 minutes, with a 10-minute break in between.

To get as much as we can out of these tests, we need your help with a few things:

- **Take notes.** Please make notes about anything interesting you notice, particularly points where the user was confused or couldn't get the tasks done. We'll be comparing notes during the debriefing session at lunchtime today.

- **Make a list at the end of each session.** During the break between sessions, use the attached sheet to jot down the three most serious usability problems you noticed in that session.

- **Come to the debriefing. (Free lunch!)** If at all possible, we'd love to have you join us at __ pm in room _____, where we'll compare notes and decide which usability problems we're going to fix in the next month.

- **If you think of a question you'd like to ask the participant, write it down.** Near the end of each session, we'll check to see if you have any questions.

- **Stay as long as you can.** We know you have other commitments, but there are only a few sessions, and each one will offer different lessons. Even if you start to lose interest, try to keep watching and listening—you never know when the participant will say something revealing. You can come and go if you need to, but please try to do it unobtrusively

- **Try to avoid distracting others.** Following a test can require concentration. Try to limit your conversation to what you're observing. If you need to have another kind of discussion or answer a phone call, please step outside the room. Think of it as a movie theater: don't talk loud enough or long enough that the people around you can't follow the plot.

Thanks for your help!

Top Three Usability Problems

After each test session, list the three most serious usability problems you noticed.

Participant #1

1. ....

2. ....

3. ....

Participant #2

1. ....

2. ....

3. ....

Participant #3

1. ....

2. ....

3. ....

The observation room

A conference room is usually ideal for the observers. If you outgrow the conference room, you can use a training room or a small auditorium—anywhere that people can see the screen and hear the audio.

One important consideration: the observation room and the test room should not be right next to each other. You don't want the participants to hear group laughter (or collective groans) that are in synch with what they've just done. Very bad.

From test room
(page 65)

a **Computer**   b **Projector**   c **Speakers**   d **Snacks**   e **Speakerphone**

a) **A computer with Internet access and screen sharing client software.**
The **computer** can be a laptop or desktop, PC or Mac, and you'll need
Internet access for screen sharing. For some kinds of **screen sharing
software** you'll have to install a viewer, but many—including GoToMeeting
—use a Web browser, so no installation is necessary.

b) The image from the **projector (**or **large screen monitor)** needs to be
large enough and bright enough so everyone can follow what the participant is doing. This is less crucial if you're testing something the observers
are very familiar with, but if you're testing new designs, competitors' sites,
or pages with dynamic content, observers will need to be able to see the
screen in some detail.

People sitting farthest from the screen will often find it easier to watch the
session on their laptops, but you have to be wary of people drifting off into
the world of email.

c) **A pair of powered speakers.** For the same reason you
want a good microphone in the test room, you want good
speakers for the observers. I recommend the Logitech
X-140 powered speakers, which cost about $25. They're
quite clear and loud and have their own volume control.

d) **Snacks.** One excellent way to make the observation
room pleasant and inviting so people will want
to come back is to provide food. Don't scrimp on
snacks! Think of them as a lure: What kind of food
is most likely to attract the Web team at 9 a.m.?
Bagels and muffins are usually a good bet, but you
should follow the local customs. If your team
is partial to granola bars and Twizzlers, give them
granola bars and Twizzlers.

e) **A speakerphone.** You should have a speakerphone available as a backup,
and make sure that you have the phone number for the test room.

Appoint a hall monitor

Since you're going to be busy in the test room, it's highly advisable to have someone minding the store for you in the observation room. Just ask someone who's planning on attending anyway and who won't mind pitching in—preferably someone who isn't easily intimidated by co-workers and bosses.

Here's a page of instructions you can give to your hall monitor:

Hall Monitor's Guide

Thanks for helping out with today's usability tests!

Since I'll be in the test room with the participants, I need your help making sure things run smoothly in the observation room.

Here's what you can do:

- Read the *Instructions for Usability Test Observers* so you know what observers need to do.

- Make sure that everyone gets a copy of the handouts as they arrive:

  - *Instructions for Usability Test Observers*
  - The test script
  - The scenarios for the tasks the participants will be doing

- Make sure everyone can see and hear the test. If there's a problem with the screen sharing or the audio, try to troubleshoot it. If you can't get it working right away, call me in the test room at _____. I'll stop the test and help you fix it.

- Try to head off any extended off-topic conversations, which can interfere with people's ability to concentrate on the test. (Limited conversation about what's happening in the test room is fine.)

- Remind people to step outside if they need to take phone calls. (Usually all you have to do is make eye contact with them and point to the door—with a smile, of course—as they put the phone to their ear.)

- As soon as each session ends, remind everyone to go back through their notes and jot down the top three problems they noticed during the test. And if they can't come to the debriefing, ask them to leave their list of problems with you.

FAQ

Aren't people's "feelers" likely to get hurt?

People ask about this a lot: Isn't it going to be painful for team members to watch people struggle—and possibly fail—while trying to use something they had a hand in building? In front of their peers and perhaps their bosses, no less? Aren't people likely to get defensive, disheartened, and even worried about losing their jobs when they see participants having trouble?

In my experience, it's usually not a serious problem.

Watching the first round of testing of your site can be a bit of a shock, which is why I recommend doing your first tests on competitors' sites, where the team members have nothing personal at stake and they can even indulge in a bit of harmless therapeutic *schadenfreude.*[2]

Most people realize quickly that even though testing exposes problems, more often than not it also suggests the solution—sometimes to a problem they've been wrestling with for a long time.

The only time I think team members are really troubled by testing is when it's done so late in the development process that there's no time to fix the problems that are uncovered. But you're not going to do that.

If you feel that there are some bruised egos on your team after testing, you may want to go out of your way to say something at the debriefing to make them feel better, like "We saw some problems, but by and large, the thing worked remarkably well. And I think the problems we saw are quite fixable."

Should people who can't observe in person be allowed to view the sessions remotely via screen sharing?

It depends: is it that they *can't* observe in person or that they don't feel like it? People who really want to watch the sessions but are legitimately unable to (because they're in another city, for instance) should certainly be allowed to. But I wouldn't recommend giving people who are on-site the option of watching at their desks instead of coming to the observation

---

[2] *Pleasure derived from the misfortunes of others.*

room. For one thing, it means they're not going to contribute to the group experience. More significantly, though, if they're at their desk (and their computer), it's going to be almost impossible for them to resist the siren song of multitasking, which means they're not going to be paying enough attention to get much value out of "watching."

Can observers be in the same room as the participant?

I don't recommend it. Experienced facilitators can manage it if necessary, but it's not a good idea for beginners.

Most participants are perfectly capable of ignoring an observer (or even two or three) in the same room with them. It's the *observers* who are the problem. Inevitably, some people just can't keep their mouths shut, and nothing can ruin a session like a manager who can't refrain from asking marketing questions or a developer who's dead set on getting the participant's opinion about a new feature he's thinking of adding.

If for some reason you have to have observers in the test room, introduce them to the participant and explain why they're there. And make it crystal clear to the observers that they *must* follow some rules:

- Be quiet. Turn off your cell phone and speak *only* when spoken to.

- Don't answer any questions the participant asks unless the facilitator specifically tells you to. Even then, keep your answer short and only answer the specific question that was asked.

- Maintain a poker face. No frowning *or* smiling and no laughing unless the participant says something clearly meant to be funny. And above all, no sighing.

- Don't coach or help the participant in any way. No nodding or grinning when they do something right, for instance.

10

Debriefing 101

COMPARING NOTES AND DECIDING WHAT TO FIX

There are some men here to flood the bed for skating.

— MR. MACGREGOR, ATTTEMPTING
TO WAKE ROBERT BENCHLEY[1]

The debriefing session has a very clearly defined purpose. You want to come out of the room with two things:

- A list of the most serious usability problems that participants encountered while using your site.

- A list of the problems you're going to fix before next month's round of testing.

The debriefing should take place as soon as possible after the test sessions while what happened is still fresh in everyone's mind.

If possible, I recommend that you make it a rule that only people who have attended at least one of the morning's test sessions can come to the debriefing. It's the price people have to pay to have a say in the meeting.

I realize that this may not be something you can enforce in your organization, and please don't get yourself fired over it. But it really is one of the best ways to ensure that people will come to the test sessions. It also helps keep the debriefing focused on what people actually observed during the tests so it doesn't devolve into "religious debates" based on personal opinions.

An hour is probably a good length for the meeting. Serve lunch, and don't scrimp: get the *good* pizza.

---

[1] *Robert Benchley was a seminal American humorist who wrote hundreds of columns for* The New Yorker *in the 1920s and '30s (many subsequently published in collections with titles like* David Copperfield, *or* Twenty Thousand Leagues Under the Sea). *If you laughed at something recently, it was probably in some way touched by Benchley's legacy. (Dave Barry has called Benchley "my idol," for instance.) Mr. MacGregor was Benchley's personal assistant, who was forced to resort to various ruses to get him out of bed in the morning.*

Take the worst first

The most important thing you need to understand about fixing usability problems is that the following statements are all true:

1. All sites have usability problems.

2. All organizations have limited resources to devote to fixing usability problems.

3. You'll always have more problems than you have the resources to fix.

4. It's easy to get distracted by less serious problems that are easier to solve, which means the worst ones often persist.

Therefore:

5. You have to be *intensely focused* on fixing the most serious problems *first*.

And yes, it's a maxim:

 **Focus ruthlessly on only the most serious problems.**

If you don't follow this rule, I can almost guarantee that the worst usability problems will still be there a month from now. And six months from now.

How do you know which problems are the most serious?

Take my word for it: it's usually pretty obvious which ones are the worst. That's one of the best things about usability testing. If you actually watch people use your site, you'll know which problems are bad.

There are basically two considerations that determine severity:

- Will a lot of people experience this problem?

- Will it cause a serious problem for the people who experience it, or is it just an inconvenience?

So, for instance, some problems are important to fix because even though they affect only a relatively small number of people, when they do they're a source of real *tsuris*.[2] (For example, the user might be unable to complete a transaction.)

Determining severity is always a judgment call. Problems that are going to cause a lot of people a lot of trouble are no-brainers. The toughest decisions involve corner cases (very damaging problems that affect only a few users) and ubiquitous nuisances (things that affect a lot of people but are really only minor annoyances).

How to run the debriefing meeting

The person running the tests (i.e., you) should run the debriefing. Here's what you do:

1. Begin by explaining how the meeting is going to work.

   "From your lists of usability problems that you observed during the test sessions we're going to choose the ten most serious ones. Then we're going to prioritize them and agree on which ones we're going to commit to fixing in the next month."

2. Ask everyone to review the list of problems they wrote down during the test sessions and choose the three that they think are the most serious.

3. Go around the room and ask people to read their three problems aloud. (If they have one that's already been mentioned, they can just say "I had _____, too.")

---

[2] *Yiddish for distress, woe, or misery. A wonderful word.*

4. Write them all down on an easel pad,[3] taping sheets up on the wall as they get full. (Leave some room between items so you can add variations suggested by others.)

5. When everyone has had a chance to contribute their three problems, look at the list and choose what seem to be the ten most serious.

   You can ask people to vote if you want, but don't be afraid to just say, "It sounded to me like these are the top ten" as you put checkmarks next to them. Then wait for any objections and make changes if necessary.

6. Write down a new rank-ordered list of these top ten problems, starting with the most serious. Leave some room between them where you'll make notes about how to fix them.

   Again, use your own judgment about the order, but listen to any reasonable suggestions about changes.

7. Working down the list without skipping any, have the team discuss briefly how each problem can be fixed within the next month. Try to keep the proposed fixes as simple as possible (see Chapter 11).

8. Continue working your way down the list until you feel like you've committed all the resources you have available for fixing things in the next month, then stop.

---

[3] *Feel free to use your list-making weapon of choice. But a whiteboard may turn out to be too small, and while a laptop connected to a projector has a lot of advantages it probably won't allow everyone to see the entire list at once.*

Tips for success

Here are some suggestions for getting the most out of the debriefing:

- Write a few guidelines on the easel pad before you begin:

  > Stick to what you observed.
  > Focus on the most serious problems.
  > Objective: a list of problems we'll fix in the next month.

- It's your meeting, so don't be afraid to run it. Encourage participation, but be clear that it's not a democracy. You're in charge, by virtue of the fact that you're (presumably) the person in the room who knows the most about usability.

- Have a laptop available with the recordings of the sessions in case you want to check anything.

- You don't have a lot of time, so keep people on track. Briefly stated opinions are fine, but don't let it degenerate into "religious debates." Keep bringing the discussion back to what they actually observed. "Are you saying that because of something you saw in the tests?" "Did anybody in the tests have that problem?"

- Run a clean meeting. Acknowledge every contribution. No belittling allowed.

- When working your way down the list and discussing fixes for the top ten problems, *don't skip any of them*. The point is, since these are some of your most serious usability problems you should be doing *something* about all of them. You don't need perfect and permanent fixes—and in fact you want to do as little as you can—but you need to do something.

  You'll often hear people say things like "Yes, that's a big problem for users, but it's going to go away next month [or next year] when we roll out Project Overlord. So there's no point in putting effort into fixing it now."

  Always treat these claims with a certain amount of skepticism.

We all know that in the real world there's always a more-than-reasonable chance that Project Overlord will end up getting delayed, scrapped, or modified beyond recognition. And even if it does come to pass, estimates of when it will happen are almost always optimistic. In the meantime, the problem exists and will continue to cause your users grief.

Rather than buy into this, ask, "What's the smallest change we can make right now that will at least smooth over this problem for most people?"

The small, non-honkin' report

After the debriefing, it's a good idea to summarize this month's testing in a short email. By short, I mean it should take no more than two minutes to read—and no more than 30 minutes to write. Think bullet points, not paragraphs. It should cover

- What you tested

- The list of tasks the participants did

- The list of problems you're going to fix in the next month as a result of what you observed

Let people know how they can watch the recordings or clips if they're interested and when the next tests will be.

FAQ

Are there other ways to run the debriefing? I've been in sessions where there were an awful lot of Post-its being stuck up on big boards....

Yes, there are many ways to skin this particular cat. Basically, you have a lot of people's observations and opinions, and you need to merge them into something resembling a consensus about next actions. It's a classic business problem, so people have come up with a lot of different ways to do it.

Do whatever works in your context. Just don't lose sight of the fact that the outcome of the meeting should be a commitment to fixing the most serious problems.

Are you saying I can't fix things like typos because they're not the worst problems?

No, you can and hopefully will fix many other usability problems based on things you noticed during the tests. Feel free to keep your own list of problems and fix them yourself or pass them on to others who can fix them. The purpose of the debriefing, though, is to make sure your finite resources are focused on the most serious problems first.

11

The least you can do™

WHY DOING LESS IS OFTEN THE BEST WAY TO FIX THINGS

Here's the most important thing I've learned over the years about fixing the problems you discover in a usability test:

When fixing problems, try to do the least you can do.

This means that when you're deciding how to fix a usability problem, the question you should always be asking is

"What's the smallest, simplest change we can make that's likely to keep people from having the problem we observed?"

But I find that people often resist this idea. Once they get into a debriefing, they find all kinds of reasons not to do as little as possible:

- **"If we're going to fix it, we want to do it right."** People seem to think that fixing a usability problem means finding a complete and permanent solution: "Eliminate the problem." I tend to take a much more pragmatic view: "Make it better for our users right now." To me, this is a case where the perfect is the enemy of the good.[1]

---

[1] *Yes, I do know that a more literal translation of Voltaire's "Le mieux est l'ennemi du bien" is probably "The best is the enemy of the good." Thanks, though. It's always nice to know people are paying attention.*

Quick fix	"Doing it right"
A lot fewer people will experience the problem	Almost no one will experience the problem
Easy to implement	May require a lot of work
Probably done in a few days	May take weeks, months, or longer

And, of course, if you implement the quick fix you can always continue to work on the "perfect" solution, but in the meantime you don't just stand there: you do something. As General Patton said, "A good plan implemented today is better than a perfect plan implemented tomorrow."[2]

- **"It's a core problem. There's no easy way to fix it."** People seem to believe that solutions to serious problems can't be simple. I think there's often some cognitive dissonance involved: "If it was easy to fix, we would have done it a long time ago."

  You may not be able to fix the root cause of a serious usability problem right away, but there's almost always *something* you can do to mitigate its impact on your users, even if the fix amounts to putting lipstick on the proverbial pig. (Or in some cases, another coat of lipstick.)

- **"That's all going to change soon anyway. We can live with it until then."** Often people will try to avoid having to do anything about a problem by pointing out that it's going to be fixed (or made irrelevant) by an upcoming redesign. Maybe *you* can live with it in the meantime, but what about your users? And what if the redesign gets delayed—or canceled?

---

[2] *I can't believe I'm actually quoting General Patton.*

Don't wait for a redesign to fix serious problems.[3] If it's a serious problem, you need to deal with it as soon as possible so it doesn't go on causing people trouble. Yes, if the redesign actually happens, you may have some duplication of effort, but you're going to keep the initial effort very small anyway.

- **"It's going to end up feeling like a kludge."** *Kludge* is such an onomatopoetic word[4]—it sounds so ugly and unpleasant. And there *can* be something distasteful about implementing a lot of temporary fixes, patches, and workarounds. But even though a piece of duct tape covering a hole in your pants may not be pretty, it's still better than a hole.

- **"We can't fix that right now. We don't have time."** It's true that you may not have time to implement the perfect solution, but for the most serious problems you always have time to do *something*. That's why when you're going through your team's list of the top ten problems, you have to start with the worst first and not skip any. These are the WORST problems. You either have to make time or find a simple, elegant way to reduce the impact of the problem on your users.

Here are the two principles for doing as little as possible that I find work best:

- Tweak, don't redesign.

- Take something away.

---

[3] *Recently, we renovated our kitchen. For ten years we'd been living with vintage grey Formica countertops (the kind with gold speckles in it) and an area rug covering the gap in the flooring where we'd taken out a back hallway to make more room. We now realize in retrospect that we could have spent $1,000 ten years ago on new linoleum and Home Depot countertops and enjoyed a better quality of life (at least in our kitchen) for an entire decade. Of course, we didn't because we knew we were going to redesign "soon," so why throw money away?*

[4] *I don't know about you, but I'm impressed. I spelled "onomatopoetic" correctly without looking it up.*

Tweak, don't redesign

When you're trying to figure out how to fix usability problems, there's always a temptation to make changes that go beyond the problems you actually observed— to redesign your whole site, your Home page, your navigation system, your whole checkout or registration system, or your whole...anything—even when what's really needed (and what you can afford to do) is some tweaks.

If you look back on the first page of this chapter, you'll notice that I didn't say your fix should keep people from having the problem. I said it should keep people from having the problem you *observed*.

I said it this way because the observed problems so often get restated as a larger problem: "He had trouble with that menu" becomes "We need to redesign our menu system."

Nine reasons why tweaking is better than redesigning

1. Tweaks cost less.

2. Tweaks require less work.

3. Tweaks don't ruin lives, break up families, and wreck careers.

4. Small changes can be made sooner.

5. Small changes are more likely to actually happen.

6. If you make larger changes, you're more likely to break other things that are working fine in the process.

7. Most people don't like change, so a redesign annoys them.

8. A redesign means making a lot of changes at once, with the attendant complexities and risks.

9. A redesign means involving a lot of people in a lot of meetings. Enough said.

The idea of a redesign can be very seductive in the abstract: it promises a new lease on life, a chance to start over and do it right this time.

In some ways making tweaks isn't as satisfying as redesigning something—in the same way repairing your old car isn't as satisfying as getting a new one. (You don't get that "new site smell," for instance.)

But tweaks do have a lot of benefits (see box on previous page).

So what *are* tweaks, anyway? Let's see. Hmmm. If only there was some quick way to look up something like that.... Oh, wait:

Tweaking

From Wikipedia, the free encyclopedia

Tweaking refers to fine-tuning or adjusting a complex system, usually an electronic device. Tweaks are any small modifications intended to improve a system.

A tweak is a slight adjustment or modification, often one that requires a few rounds of trial and error to get it exactly right.

Usually Web site tweaks involve making something more prominent by changing its size, position, or appearance, changing some wording, or just moving things around.

Here's the process, which is also shown in the flowchart on the next page:

1. Try a simple tweak first: the simplest change you can make that you think might solve the observed problem for most people.

2. If it doesn't seem to work, try a stronger version of the same tweak. For instance, if you tried making something larger, try making it a little larger. Keep trying until either (a) it feels done or (b) it's clear that it's not going to work.

3. If the first tweak doesn't work, consider trying another, different tweak before turning to redesign.

4. Always keep an eye out for unintended consequences. Does it seem like your change has thrown something else out of whack? (As the old saying goes, if it ain't broke, don't break it.)

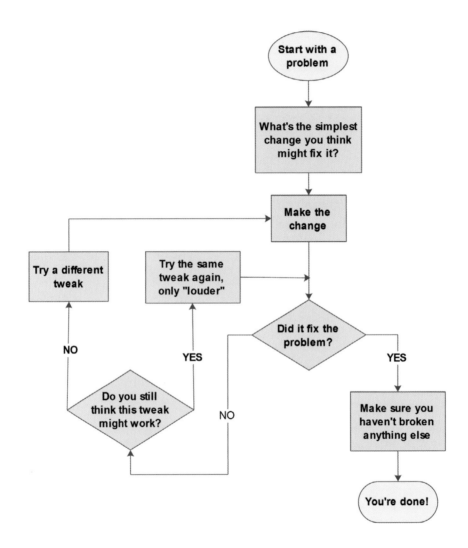

Take something away

One of the things people are often tempted to do when there's a usability problem is to add something. If someone didn't understand the instructions, add more instructions. If someone couldn't find what they were looking for in the text, add more text. If someone didn't notice something they needed to, add more color to it, or make it bolder, or make it larger.

But very often the best way to fix a usability problem is to do just the opposite: take something away. Remove something from the page.

The real problem very often is that there's already too much there. Most pages have all kinds of things that the user doesn't need: too many words, too many irrelevant pictures, too much decoration—too much "noise"—and that's the reason users aren't finding what they need.

If your first impulse is to add something, you should always question it. Usually you're better off taking away some of the things that were distracting the user.

As French aviator, adventurer, and author Antoine de Saint-Exupéry said, "A designer knows he has achieved perfection not when there is nothing left to add, but when there is nothing left to take away."

FAQ

Don't you need to do a redesign sometimes?

Redesign? Yes. All-at-once, redone-from-the-ground-up redesign? Maybe.

For a while periodic redesigns were considered a necessity, just like new car models every year. They didn't really have to be better than last year's, just new. But the current trend seems to be away from wholesale redesign and toward phased, continuous redesign. In fact, Jared Spool has gone so far as to say he's never seen a major redesign that's worked.

How do you know if your tweaks worked? Do you retest the same tasks the following month to make sure?

I used to think retesting your fixes was always necessary. In fact, I used to glibly paraphrase Ronald Reagan: "Tweak, but verify."

If you make a major change or a lot of smaller changes as a result of what you saw in testing, you may want to include the same task in the next monthly round of testing.

But the truth is, not an awful lot of retesting goes on and not a lot is necessary, because you can usually tell just by looking at it that the tweak is an effective one. When you look at the tweaked page, you usually get a pretty clear sense of either "This solves that problem" or "This doesn't solve that problem." To coin a phrase, it's not rocket surgery.

Usually it will be obvious that the new, improved version is better and fixes the problem. If you're not entirely certain, though, you have a few options:

- **Do a few quick "hallway tests."** Often what you're trying to verify is along the lines of "People didn't notice the left-hand navigation. Will they notice it now that we've made it more prominent?" Grab almost anybody, give them the scenario for the affected task (or even a simplified version that focuses on the thing that was changed), and ask them to think aloud and do the task.

- **Test it with a remote testing service like Usertesting.com (page 138–139).** Submit the URL of the tweaked version and the relevant task and pay for one or two users to try doing it.

- **Run an A/B test of the original and tweaked versions.** Using something like Google Website Optimizer (available free as part of Google Analytics), you can run a test that sends half of your site visitors to the original page and half to your tweaked version. Then it allows you to see, for instance, whether more people who used the tweaked version actually got to whatever target page you intended them to get to.

12

The usual suspects

SOME PROBLEMS YOU'RE LIKELY TO FIND AND HOW TO
THINK ABOUT FIXING THEM

W hen you do a lot of usability testing, you tend to see the same problems turn up over and over.

You'd think it would get boring, but somehow it doesn't. In fact, over time you develop favorites, and they're a little like old friends. You're always glad to see them again—like the marine biologists who recognize individual whales returning each year by the patterns and scars on their flukes, or the prisoners who know each others' jokes so well they tell them by number.[1]

I thought it might be helpful to talk about two of my personal favorites—which I also happen to think are among the ones that cause the most trouble—and explain how I think about fixing them.

Say hello for me when you see them. (You will.)

---

[1] *A man goes to prison. Every so often somebody calls out a number, like "42," and all the other prisoners laugh uproariously. He asks his cellmate what's going on. "We've all heard the same jokes so often that we gave them numbers," he explains. "If you want to tell a joke, you just call out the number."*

Eventually the newcomer screws up his courage and calls out "37." Nobody laughs. "What happened?" he asks. His cellmate shrugs and says, "Some people just can't tell a joke."

Getting off on the wrong foot

THE PROBLEM:

The usability problem that has always fascinated me the most is users getting off on the wrong foot.

When you watch a usability test, you're basically watching somebody take a little trip. They figure out where they want to go, they get their bearings, and then they head out. You're standing by, just watching; you can see their every move—and even hear their thought process—but you can't help them.

What amazes me most is *how often* people get off on the wrong foot. Time and again you'll see people start off with some misapprehension and head off in all kinds of wrong directions, often without realizing for a long time that they're in any trouble.

It's exactly like what Erik Jonsson describes in his wonderful book about how people get lost, *Inner Navigation* (Scribner, 2007).

On a trip to Cologne in 1948, Jonsson left the train station before dawn and headed toward the Rhine. He was sure he was heading west, even though he could see the sun rising over the river ahead of him. He remained "turned around," thinking that east was west and vice versa, until he finally left the city. He spent years afterwards collecting stories about how people have gotten lost, trying to figure out how it happens.

It turns out that the first steps are crucial: people who start off lost tend to stay lost. If you think you know where you're going but you really don't, it's easy to end up wandering around aimlessly.

I've come to think of it in terms of what I call the Big Bang Theory of Web Usability. Like the real Big Bang, a lot happens in your first few seconds on a new Web page or Web site:

- You take in an overall impression, mostly visual: Does it look professional? Polished? Serious? Reliable? An excellent research paper ("Attention Web Designers: You Have 50 Milliseconds to Make a Good First Impression!"[2]) makes a convincing argument that this process happens *very* quickly.

- You parse the page visually, identifying the regions of the page and making assumptions about what's where.

- You identify the site: What is it? Who publishes it? What kinds of things are here? And so on.

In other words, you form a number of working assumptions, which may or may not be accurate. You use those first bits of information you acquire ("This is a ___ site") as a toehold, the Rosetta Stone that you use to help interpret everything you see later. If your assumptions are wrong, you'll try to force everything you see to fit them, usually creating *more* misinterpretations that have to be straightened out. The lost get...loster.

As a Web designer, you've got to make sure your site sets users off on the right foot. Do visitors get the big picture: what this is, how it's organized, what they can find here and what they can do here? And do they get it in a few seconds, with little or no effort?

---

[2] *Gitte Lindgaard, Gary Fernandes, Cathy Dudek and J. Brown,* Behaviour & Information Technology, *Vol. 25, No. 2, March-April 2006, 115–126.*

HOW TO THINK ABOUT FIXING IT:

People get lost on sites for a lot of reasons, but the thing that most often gets them off on the wrong foot is a failure of the Home page to do its job of orienting them. You have to make sure your Home page works.

And even a good Home page requires constant vigilance.

The user experience of Home pages, in particular, has a tendency to deteriorate over time as stakeholders insist on adding things. As a result, most Home pages suffer from the kitchen sink syndrome: just too much *stuff*. (When I look at most Home pages—overcrowded, no focus, in my face—I feel a little bit like the boy in *The Sixth Sense*, except that instead of "I see dead people," the thought going through my head is "I see stakeholders.")

You need to check regularly to make sure that your Home page still works, which is why I think it's always worth doing a Home page tour in every test session. You can never test your Home page too many times. (And besides: it never hurts to have everyone on the team—particularly stakeholders—hear strangers say, "There's an awful lot here. I'm not sure what all of this stuff is.")

Failure to shout

THE PROBLEM:

Designers—especially designers who have ever worked in print—love subtle visual distinctions. In print, for instance, you can use a hairline rule to indicate one kind of heading and a half-point rule to indicate another, and people may actually notice the difference. (More important, judges in design competitions will notice the difference.) And things like hairline rules and tiny, low-contrast type are hallmarks of sophisticated design.

Unfortunately, people using the Web are moving so fast—and screen resolution is so low compared to print—that they almost always miss subtle visual distinctions. Web users rarely "get" subtle visual cues.

HOW TO THINK ABOUT FIXING IT:

If it's important that people notice something on your site, you need to make it stand out more than you probably think you do—and almost certainly more than your visual designer would like.

What you and your designer need to understand is that this doesn't mean it has to be ugly.

For instance, on the page on the right, what do you think are the two things Amazon has decided their visitors *absolutely* need to notice?

I'm guessing you knew it was the two yellow buttons. I'm guessing it because I've shown this page many times in my slides and people usually have no trouble spotting the buttons from 50 or 75 feet away.

Here's another example, from a site the Usability Professionals Association built a few years ago for World Usability Day. As you might imagine, it was quite...usable. The top of the page looked like this:

But if they actually wanted people to notice and use the excellent navigation system they'd built, the visual cues that would let you know it was there needed to be less subtle. Here's a version I doctored to show what I mean:

If you want people to use something you've built, they have to notice it first. I think it's always possible to maintain visual appeal—and even sophisticated design—and still direct people's attention to where it needs to be.

FAQ

Why so much focus on the Home page? Hasn't Google made it irrelevant?

There's no question that nowadays most of us *live* in Google. Almost everything I do starts with a Google search. Or a Wikipedia search.

In fact, I even use Google to do my Wikipedia searches. For instance, I type "Hasselhoff wiki" in Google, and sure enough, the first entry on the Google results page is the Wikipedia page for David Hasselhoff. Nine times out of ten it's what I was looking for.

As a result many (or most) of the people who come to your site don't enter via your Home page anymore. They search for something in Google and go directly to some lower-level page in your site.

A lot of people think this means that the Home page is no longer important, but they're wrong.

If people land on an interior page of a site and it's not exactly what they're looking for, very often the next thing they'll do is look around for a Home link so they can bob up to the surface and get their bearings. What is this site all about? Who are these people? What else do they have to offer? Are they credible? Very often, their next click after that is on an About Us link, and hopefully, the About Us page starts with a clear, simple, brief explanation of who the publisher of the site is and what they do—and not a mission statement.

The Home page still matters and its job is to clarify who you are and what you do quickly, so people who teleported in via Google can decide whether your site is worth further exploration.

13

Making sure life actually improves

THE ART OF PLAYING NICELY WITH OTHERS

Interviewer: *But do you feel you've learned from your mistakes?*

Sir Arthur Streeb-Greebling: *I think I have, yes. I'm sure I could repeat them exactly.*

—PETER COOKE AND DUDLEY MOORE, IN THEIR "FROG AND PEACH" SKETCH

While writing this book, I looked back through a lot of reports from tests I facilitated years ago for clients. I used to do very nice versions (if I do say so myself) of the Big Honkin' Report, complete with screenshots illustrating the problems and sometimes even some doctored screenshots showing possible solutions. They were very clear and easy to read (I was told), and my clients seemed to agree strongly with my conclusions. In fact, they were usually very enthusiastic about the process and jazzed about the idea of improving their product.

But then I'd watch their sites for signs of the fixes being implemented. And a disappointing number of times, nothing happened. Three months. Six months. A year. Nothing.

Even though my reports typically mentioned dozens of problems, I always tried to make a clear list of the most serious ten or fifteen and emphasize that these should be given top priority.

Some of these problems involved relatively easy to implement fixes that I thought would make a huge improvement in the site's customer experience, and quite probably in its profitability. And the people I delivered my findings to (often fairly high up the organizational food chain) agreed that the changes were important and valuable. Even though the problems I was talking about usually weren't news to the people who brought me into the project, they *were* news to those higher up, and they seemed clearly committed to making the fixes soon.

I've seen this happen many times in all kinds of organizations, and other usability professionals have told me that they've often had similar experiences.

Why things don't get fixed

So what's going on? If people understand what the serious problems are and how to fix them and they have the requisite clout to make sure it gets done—and in many cases the problems aren't even very hard to fix—why don't things improve?

Why does this happen? And more important, how can you make sure it doesn't happen to you? Here are some of the usual reasons why things end up not getting fixed:

- Change of management, change of direction, or both.

- Putting things off. If fixing a problem turns out to be more work than anticipated, the easiest solution is to just say "That'll have to wait for our next redesign." (Translation: the check is in the mail.)

- Lack of sufficient buy-in from all the right people.

- Sabotage. Believe it or not, team members and stakeholders who feel they didn't have a voice in deciding what to fix have sometimes been known to drag their feet.

- Your eyes were bigger than your stomach. In their enthusiasm, teams often put an unrealistic number of problems on their plate.

- Problems turn out to have deep roots. When you go to fix some usability problems, it quickly becomes clear that they're actually a symptom of some much larger unresolved conflict—about the site's purpose or the company's mission, for instance.

And above all,

- Life intervenes. For whatever reason it turns out that you just don't have the time, resources, or commitment to follow through.

To survive all of these and end up with real improvement, you need serious, durable commitment from everyone involved: management, your team, and the stakeholders.

It helps to have friends in high places

People often ask me about the best way to sell usability to management.

One obvious way is to be persuasive: understand management's goals and figure out how usability can advance them, learn to speak their language, make frequent presentations about your testing efforts, and so on. Certainly a good idea.

You can also make the argument for the return on investment (ROI) for money spent on usability. There's even an excellent book on the subject: *Cost-Justifying Usability* (2nd Edition, 2005, edited by Randolph Bias and Deborah Mayhew). ROI case studies can be very convincing,[1] but they also tend to be very time-consuming and expensive to create.

And even if you succeed in convincing management, when money is tight, as the new kid on the block usability is likely to be one of the first things thrown overboard (following the last-hired/first-fired principle).

Usability testing (and user-centered design in general) is slowly (very slowly, I think) becoming a "must have" for *some* enlightened organizations. But in tough times, it's still not on the "indispensable" list.

And when it comes down to getting products out the door sooner or getting them out the door *and usable* a little later, usability will often lose. Management knows that users won't be able to do anything if you haven't got code and content written, but it's easy to assume that even if the thing is confusing or hard to use people will still manage to use it somehow.

---

[1] *...particularly when you're working on an intranet, where you can quantify the payoff. ("Our tests show that with a new design employees can save 15 minutes a week in the time they spend looking people up in our corporate directory. At an average salary of 35 cents a minute for 1,000 employees, it amounts to a savings of over $200,000 per year. Our testing and redesign cost $10,000. Net savings: $190,000.")*

Personally, I'm not a big fan of using ROI arguments. I think most companies that need ROI-style proof to convince them to "do usability" probably aren't going to do great work anyway. That requires more than the sense that it's profitable—it requires a passion to do it right. Buy-in is OK in flush times, but when resources are short, you need people who are fanatics—who can't imagine not spending time and money on creating a top-notch user experience.

So what works?

Fortunately, you have at your disposal a mechanism for generating conversion experiences, which is what it takes to make a fanatic.

Rather than engage in arguments about the value of testing, I'd rather rely on demonstration. Don't try to make converts: let the seeing-is-believing effect of watching usability testing make converts for you. I tend to think it's much easier and longer lasting and more recession-proof to have the boss and everyone on the team become true believers.

14

Teleportation made easy

REMOTE TESTING: FAST, CHEAP, AND SLIGHTLY OUT OF CONTROL

What am I working on?
Uhh.... I'm working on something that will
change the world, and human life as we know it.

—SETH BRUNDLE (JEFF GOLDBLUM), IN *THE FLY*

Remote testing is a simple idea: instead of bringing the users to you, you go to them—electronically. Instead of looking at the screen over the participant's shoulder, you use screen sharing. And instead of conversing face to face, you talk on the phone (or via VOIP).

I first did remote testing 15 years ago. With no screen sharing software, I had to imagine what the user was doing—based on what he said while thinking aloud—and try to duplicate his actions on my computer so I could follow along. As you might imagine, I spent a lot of time asking "What screen are you on now?"

Today, though, with robust screen sharing software and broadband access, the experience is a lot like looking over the participant's shoulder.

Why do it?

One word: convenience. Remote testing has several significant advantages:

- **Easier recruiting.** Your pool of potential participants widens from "people who live or work near where you're testing" to "anybody with a fast internet connection." This is particularly helpful when you're looking for a particular type of user.

- **No travel required.** For the participant this means the whole thing takes an hour of their time, not two. This is very helpful when recruiting people who have very little free time.

- **Easier scheduling.** You can do tests at almost any time of day. For hard to find people who are only available at 11 pm, you can run sessions at 11 pm.

- **Produces [almost] the same results.** Remote testing is very likely to uncover the same kinds and the same amount of problems as testing in person.

If it's so great, why not do *all* tests remotely?

Overall, I'd say remote testing gives you about 80% of the benefits of a live test with about 70% of the effort.[1]

You do lose 20 percent of *something* not being in the same room as the participant. The in-person experience is just richer, somehow. It's just a little harder to know exactly what they're thinking.

And having a layer of technology between you can lead to misunderstandings. It's about the same as the difference between having a conversation with someone on the phone as compared to having the same conversation in person. You usually have to spend more time clarifying what the participant said and meant.

You also have a lot less control of the session. For instance, if someone walks into the participant's office, or the participant decides to take a phone call, there's comparatively little you can do about it. And it can be particularly harder to rein in tough customers when you're not in the same room, because you can't use your body language to indicate that you *really* mean it's time to get back on track.

How do you do it?

Almost everything about remote testing is the same as testing in person: you choose what to test, write scenarios, follow the script, ask them to think aloud, probe, and so on. You can test anything you can display on the screen. You may have to make minor modifications to the script and you'll have to mail them their incentive check or email them an Amazon gift certificate.

You always need to do a quick test of the screen sharing before the test session. You can do this when you call to confirm their test appointment.

You have to decide whose screen is going to be shared: yours or theirs. It's best to let them access what you're testing from their computer while you watch via screen sharing so they won't be affected by the inevitable (but usually slight

---

[1] *Yes, that's a guesstimate. As Jared Spool like to say in presentations, "74% of all statistics in presentations are made up on the spot."*

lag time). If you're testing something that is only installed on your computer, you can give them control of your screen.

(If they're sharing their screen, be sure to tell them to hide anything they don't want you to see, like email.)

As I mentioned in Chapter 8, you have a number of options for screen sharing software. The most important factor in choosing one for remote testing is ease of use for the participants. You want something that (a) requires as little setup time for the participant as possible (preferably less than a minute), (b) will work through corporate firewalls, if necessary, and (c) doesn't require installing an actual application, which many corporate IT departments won't allow.

Again, I prefer GoToMeeting for screen sharing, and I have nothing but good things to say about it. The installation for the participant is a simple automatic download that takes about 30 seconds, and I have yet to encounter a participant who couldn't use it. It tends to refresh the screen quickly so there's little or no lag between what the participant sees and what you see.

It also does an excellent job of screen resizing (since your screen may not be the same size or resolution as the participant's), and it makes it very easy to switch whose screen is being shared.[2]

For audio, you can use GoToMeeting's conference calling service (included in the subscription price, but each caller pays their own toll call charges), or you can use VOIP if the participant has a microphone connected to his computer.

If you're not using VOIP the participant should have a speakerphone if possible, so they don't have to hold a phone to their ear for 50 minutes. Ask them to turn on call waiting if they have it and agree to try to keep interruptions to a minimum. Since they'll be at home or at work, though, you have to be prepared for interruptions.

You can record the entire session by running a screen recorder on your computer, positioning the microphone near the speakerphone.

---

[2] *I know, I know. "If you love GoToMeeting so much why don't you marry it?" But it's so well designed that I really do enjoy using it. I rarely do any kind of conference call anymore without using screen sharing.*

Faster, cheaper, and even more out of control

While we're talking about remote testing, there's one other option you should be aware of: unmoderated remote testing.[3]

Consider a service like Usertesting.com.[4] Here's how it works:

You give them a URL for what you want to test and a task (or maybe two short tasks). Then you tell them how many participants you want and specify a few preferences like gender, age, income, and computer experience.

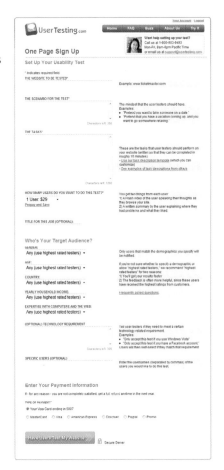

They post the request online to their pool of testers, who then sign up to do it. Each tester goes to the URL and spends about 15 minutes doing the task(s), while thinking aloud. When they're done, you get a link to a screen recording of their session.

Obviously, it's not the same as sitting down with a user, because you can't ask questions and you can't probe. But given the limitations, the recordings can be surprisingly helpful. (The participants have been screened to ensure that they're good at thinking aloud, and they tend to put a fair amount of effort into it.)

---

[3] *Tom Tullis, Bill Albert, and Donna Tedesco will be publishing a book on the topic* (Beyond the Usability Lab) *in 2010.*

[4] *There are several of them now with the same business model. Usertesting.com was one of the first and it's the one I'm most familiar with.*

The beauty of it is that it's inexpensive ($29 per user), requires very little effort (you just have to come up with the task), and fast (you can often get results back the next day).

The quality is not going to be the same as doing a moderated test, but I've been favorably impressed.

For the price, I think it's an excellent thing to have in your toolbox. It's perfect for getting a quick-and-dirty take on some question that's not worth including in your monthly testing, or that just can't wait for it. It's also very handy for doing a quick retest after you've fixed a problem you found in monthly testing, since you already have the task written.

FAQ

Why is this chapter at the end of the book?

An excellent question. It does seem like it might make more sense to have this in the "Finding Problems" section of the book. But there's a very good reason why I put it back here:

> *You shouldn't try remote testing until you have*
> *some in-person tests under your belt.*

Remote testing requires more concentration, and not having the ability to "read" the person visually is a much more significant loss for a beginner.

I'd recommend that you wait until you've done about three monthly rounds of testing before you start doing them remotely. By then, the whole process will feel much more routine and you'll be more relaxed and better able to cope with the unexpected.

(Of course, if you want, you can begin experimenting with remote testing before then. I just wouldn't do it for your public sessions.)

Should we still have an observation room?

Yes. It's just as important to have people observe remote tests as it is for in-house tests. You want that "clubhouse" effect where people compare notes and share the experience. Since they'll be observing via screen sharing in either case, from their perspective the experience will be exactly the same.

15

Overachievers only

RECOMMENDED READING

Isn't there somebody a little more qualified?

—BOBCAT GOLDTHWAIT, WHEN ASKED IF HE WANTED TO
CUT HIS NEWBORN SON'S UMBILICAL CORD

Once you've started doing some testing, some of you will want to learn more about it.[1] For the benefit of you overachievers, here are my favorite books about testing and related topics.

Books about testing in general

As I said in the introduction, I deliberately haven't tried to cover every aspect of testing in detail. These three books do just that, and they do it very well; you can't go wrong with any one of them.

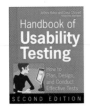

Handbook of Usability Testing (Second Edition)
Jeffrey Rubin and Dana Chisnell, John Wiley & Sons, 2008.

Jeff Rubin's book was long one of the best on the subject, and the new edition with co-author Dana Chisnell has made a very good thing even better.

A Practical Guide to Usability Testing (Revised Edition)
Joseph Dumas and Janice (Ginny) Redish, Intellect, 1999.

Between them, Joe and Ginny probably know more about usability testing than the rest of us put together, and they both make a wonderful habit of sharing what they know.

---

[1] *Some of you won't, which is fine, too. Personally, I've tried for years now to convince people that I'm really not one of those people who have limitless curiosity about things, but I've had only modest success.*

Usability Testing Essentials: Ready, Set, Test!
Carol Barnum, Longman, 2010.

As I write this, Carol is still working on this major revision of her excellent 2002 book, but I know it will be well worth reading, with new topics like accessibility and international usability testing.

Specific topics

Paper Prototyping
Carolyn Snyder, Morgan Kaufmann, 2003.

As Johnny Carson would have said, "Every *single thing* you need to know about paper prototyping is in this book." And a very good book on testing in general, too.

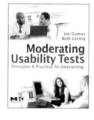

Moderating Usability Tests
Joseph Dumas and Beth Loring, Morgan Kaufmann, 2008.

An entire book—based on 40 years of combined experience—about the process of facilitating a test. A very quick and very informative read.

Measuring the User Experience
Thomas Tullis and William Albert, Morgan Kaufmann, 2008.

If you need to do some quantitative testing (for instance, if your boss insists on a benchmark test so you can "prove" your site has improved later), you *must* read this book.

Recruiting Without Fear
Will Schroeder, David Brittan, and Jared Spool. Usability Interface Engineering, 43-page downloadable PDF, $49.99
http://www.uie.com/reports

Jared Spool's company has been recruiting test participants since 1988, and this white paper explains how they do it.

233 Tips and Tricks for Recruiting Users as Participants in Usability Studies
Deborah Sova and Jakob Nielsen, Nielsen Norman Group, 144-page downloadable PDF, $79.95
http://www.nngroup.com/reports

Co-author Deborah Sova draws on years of experience as a recruiter to offer plenty of sound advice.

Books about fixing things

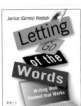

Letting Go of the Words: Writing Web Content That Works
Janice (Ginny) Redish, Morgan Kaufmann, 2007.

Ginny's book is *the* best advice available on fixing usability problems that are the result of less-than-perfect writing or editing—and avoiding them in the first place. One Web writer described it to me as "life-altering" and I think she's right.

Forms that Work: Designing Web Forms for Usability
Caroline Jarrett and Gerry Gaffney, Morgan Kaufmann, 2008.

Almost every Web site has some forms, and almost every Web form has usability problems. This book is to forms what Ginny's book is to writing.

16

Happy trails / to you

A FEW FINAL WORDS OF ENCOURAGEMENT

Here are all of my "maxims."

A morning a month, that's all we ask.

Start earlier than you think makes sense.

Recruit loosely and grade on a curve.

Make it a spectator sport.

Focus ruthlessly on a small number of the most important problems.

When fixing problems, always do the least you can do.

Keep these in mind, and you'll do fine. And remember, everything in here is just a recommendation. Feel free to experiment and do whatever works for you.

Good luck, and please let me know how you make out. (You can write to me at stevekrug@rocketsurgerymadeeasy.com.)

Sample test
script and
consent form

Test script

> ☐ **Web browser should be open to Google or some other "neutral" page**

Hi, _____. My name is _____, and I'm going to be walking you through this session today.

Before we begin, I have some information for you, and I'm going to read it to make sure that I cover everything.

You probably already have a good idea of why we asked you here, but let me go over it again briefly. We're asking people to try using a Web site that we're working on so we can see whether it works as intended. The session should take about an hour.

The first thing I want to make clear is that we're testing the *site*, not you. You can't do anything wrong here. In fact, this is probably the one place today where you don't have to worry about making mistakes.

As you use the site, I'm going to ask you as much as possible to try to think out loud: to say what you're looking at, what you're trying to do, and what you're thinking. This will be a big help to us.

Also, please don't worry that you're going to hurt our feelings. We're doing this to improve the site, so we need to hear your honest reactions.

If you have any questions as we go along, just ask them. I may not be able to answer them right away, since we're interested in how people do when they don't have someone sitting next to them to help. But if you still have any questions when we're done, I'll try to answer them then. And if you need to take a break at any point, just let me know.

You may have noticed the microphone. With your permission, we're going to record what happens on the screen and our conversation. The recording will only be used to help us figure out how to improve the site, and it won't be seen by anyone except the people working on this project. And it helps me because I don't have to take as many notes.

Also, there are a few people from the Web design team observing this session in another room. (They can't see us, just the screen.)

If you would, I'm going to ask you to sign a simple permission form for us. It just says that we have your permission to record you and that the recording will only be seen by the people working on the project.

- ☐ **Give them a recording permission form and a pen**

- ☐ **While they sign it, START the SCREEN RECORDER**

IF YOU ARE USING A NONDISCLOSURE AGREEMENT (optional):

I know we also sent you a nondisclosure agreement that says that you won't talk to anybody about what we're showing you today, since it hasn't been made public yet. Do you have that with you?

- ☐ **Accept the NDA and make sure that it's signed. If they don't have it with them, hand them a copy and give them time to read and sign it.**

Do you have any questions so far?

OK. Before we look at the site, I'd like to ask you just a few quick questions.

First, what's your occupation? What do you do all day?

Now, roughly how many hours a week altogether—just a ballpark estimate—would you say you spend using the Internet, including Web browsing and email, at work and at home?

And what's the split between email and browsing—a rough percentage?

What kinds of sites are you looking at when you browse the Web?

Do you have any favorite Web sites?

OK, great. We're done with the questions, and we can start looking at things.

☐ **Click on the bookmark for the site's Home page.**

First, I'm going to ask you to look at this page and tell me what you make of it: what strikes you about it, whose site you think it is, what you can do here, and what it's for. Just look around and do a little narrative.

You can scroll if you want to, but don't click on anything yet.

☐ **Allow this to continue for three or four minutes, at most.**

Thanks. Now I'm going to ask you to try doing some specific tasks. I'm going to read each one out loud and give you a printed copy.

I'm also going to ask you to do these tasks without using Search. We'll learn a lot more about how well the site works that way.

And again, as much as possible, it will help us if you can try to think out loud as you go along.

☐ **Hand the participant the first scenario, and read it aloud.**

☐ **Allow the user to proceed until you don't feel like it's producing any value or the user becomes very frustrated.**

☐ **Repeat for each task or until time runs out.**

Thanks, that was very helpful.

If you'll excuse me for a minute, I'm just going to see if the people on the team have any follow-up questions they'd like me to ask you.

- ☐ **Call the observation room to see if the observers have any questions.**

- ☐ **Ask the observers' question(s) and then probe about anything you want to follow up on.**

Do you have any questions for me, now that we're done?

- ☐ **Give them their incentive, or remind them it will be sent to them.**

- ☐ **Stop the screen recorder and save the file.**

- ☐ **Thank them and escort them out.**

Recording consent form

Thank you for participating in our usability research.

We will be recording your session to allow [ORGANIZATION NAME] staff members who are unable to be here today to observe your session and benefit from your comments.

Please read the statement below and sign where indicated.

- -

I understand that my usability test session will be recorded.

I grant [ORGANIZATION NAME] permission to use this recording for the purpose of improving the designs being tested.

Signature: _____

Print your name: _____

Date: _____

Acknowledgments

I have always depended on the kindness of strangers.

—BLANCHE DUBOIS IN *A STREETCAR NAMED DESIRE*

The people involved in getting this book done weren't strangers to me: I was lucky enough to be able to round up the same team that made *Don't Make Me Think* happen. But I have relied deeply on their kindness and their extraordinary patience and goodwill in the face of my writing habits.

In no particular order:

My reviewers—**Joe Dumas**, **Caroline Jarrett**, **Karen Whitehouse**, and **Paul Shakespear**—who all spent precious time to keep me from appearing foolish. To protect the innocent, I feel compelled to note that inclusion in this list does not imply agreement with everything in the book.

Elisabeth Bayle. Before Elisabeth appeared three years ago, I'd worked alone for almost 30 years and could never imagine it otherwise (largely the result of a nightmarish collaboration in the early '80s). Since then, I've had the pleasure of a colleague and a friend who knows as much about this stuff as I do. I stretch her patience constantly and we sometimes disagree, but we have a rule about not throwing things.

Barbara Flanagan, copyeditor, old friend, and grammar maven, without whom this book would have a copyright date of 2014. Any instances of things like "who" where it should be "whom" are attributable to my stubbornness and her indulgence. I would love to write a book with her about how to write.

Allison Cecil (and her Great Danes), who took time out from flattening and hand stamping 4,000 pieces of silverware into beautiful garden markers (available at Anthropologie) to design yet another book for me.

Mark Matcho, whose illustrations add so much.

Nancy Ruenzel, Nancy Davis, **Lisa Brazieal**, **Glenn Bisignani**, **Charlene Will**, and all the other smart, nice, hardworking people at Peachpit who have been so supportive (often while biting their tongues, I'm sure).

Ginny Redish and **Caroline Jarrett** for being themselves.

The large **community of usability professionals**, who tend to be a very nice bunch of folks. Go to an annual UPA conference and find out for yourself.

Randolph Bias and **Carol Barnum,** who both understand the theoretical underpinnings of this far better than I ever will and were brave enough to do a panel with me at the 2008 UPA conference titled "Discount Testing by Amateurs: Threat or Menace?"

My friends **Richard Gingras** and **Mitzi Trumbo,** who were so patient with a houseguest who was mostly stuck to his computer, writing, even in the face of a cliffside view of the Pacific.

Harry, now in college, who still manages to send me the occasional link to things that he knows will make me laugh.

And finally, **Melanie,** for being supportive even when she insisted she wasn't. As Richard Fariña said in one of the "Little Nothing Poems" he wrote for Mimi, "Nothing matters / any more."[1]

---

[1] *Just in case it's not clear (and I have to admit that poetry is often not clear to* me*), there's an implied "than you" at the end:*

Nothing matters
any more [than you].

Index

T

target audience, 40
tasks, 51, 76
testing, do-it-yourself vs. Big Honkin',
   24–26
testing things besides Web sites, 11
test room, 65–67
The least you can do™, 110–119
things you can say, 83–84
tweaking, 114–116
   confirming success of, 118

U

usability professionals
   advantages of using, 6
Usability Professionals' Association
   (UPA), 7
usability testing
   defined, 13
   do-it-yourself. *See* do-it-yourself
      usability testing
   quantitative, 13
   why it works, 16
   why so little gets done, 18
Usertesting.com, 138–39

V

VOIP (voice over IP), 67, 137

W

what to test, 31–37
when to test, 31–32
where to test, 65–67
who to test with, 39–49
wireframes, testing, 36

STEVE KRUG
did his first usability
test twenty years ago,
and he still learns
something new every
time he does one.

MARK MATCHO
has been an illustrator
for twenty years,
and has pretty much
worked for every dern magazine
out there, at one point or another.
His work can be found in this book,
and at markmatcho.net.

This book was produced digitally
using Microsoft Word, Adobe
Photoshop, and Adobe Illustrator.
Layout and production were
accomplished using Adobe
InDesign. Files were passed
among all parties concerned
and were proofed using Adobe
Acrobat. The text face is Farnham.
The chapter titles and paragraph
headings were set in MetaPlus,
designed by Erik Spiekermann.
All captions were set in FF Letter
Gothic Text, designed by Albert
Pinggera.

WATCH
READ
CREATE

Unlimited online access to all Peachpit, Adobe Press, Apple Training and New Riders videos and books, as well as content from other leading publishers including: O'Reilly Media, Focal Press, Sams, Que, Total Training, John Wiley & Sons, Course Technology PTR, Class on Demand, VTC and more.

No time commitment or contract required! Sign up for one month or a year.
All for $19.99 a month

SIGN UP TODAY
peachpit.com/creativeedge